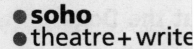

C000225236

Soho Theatre Company presents

A Night at the Dogs

by Matt Charman

Winner of the Verity Bargate Award 2004

First performed at Soho Theatre on 8 April 2005

Soho Theatre is supported by

 gettyimages

Performances in the Lorenz Auditorium

Registered Charity No: 267234

A Night at the Dogs

by Matt Charman

CARL CRASSMAN	NEIL STUKE
DANNY CRASSMAN	JOE ARMSTRONG
CHALKY	MARK HADFIELD
LIONEL	TREVOR COOPER
PAUL	DAVID HOUNSLOW
SHARKEY'S NECKLACE	BONNIE, JEDDA, JENNY, KAY, MOLLY, SLY, TEO, TRILBY

Director	Abigail Morris
Assistant Director	James Hammond
Designer	Michael Vale
Lighting Designer	Ben Ormerod
Sound Designer	Kay Basson
Production Manager	Nick Ferguson
Stage Manager	Sarah Buik
Deputy Stage Manager	Laura Flowers
Prop Buyer	Esther Armstrong
Costume Supervisor	Frances Pinney
Chief Technician	Nick Blount
Chief Electrician	Christoph Wagner
Lighting Technician	Mark Watts
Built and painted by	Capital Scenery
Press Representation	Nancy Poole (020 7478 0142)
Photography	Getty Images

Soho Theatre and Writers' Centre
21 Dean St, London W1D 3NE

Admin: 020 7287 5060 *Fax:* 020 7287 5061 *Box Office:* 0870 429 6883
www.sohotheatre.com   *email:* box@sohotheatre.com

Biographies

Writer

Matt Charman *Writer*

Matt won the Verity Bargate Award 2004, the national new writing competition, for *A Night at the Dogs*. He is Writer-in-Residence at Soho Theatre and has just been commissioned to write his second play.

Cast

Joe Armstrong *Danny Crassman*

Joe's theatre credits include *Protection* (Soho Theatre) and *How Love is Spelt* (Bush Theatre). Television credits include *Midsomer Murders* (Bentley Productions); *Foyle's War* (Greenlit Productions); *Blackpool, Waking the Dead, Passer By* (BBC); *Between the Sheets* (Rollem Productions) and *The Bill* (Thames).

Trevor Cooper *Lionel*

Trevor's recent theatre credits include *By the Bog of Cats* (Wyndhams Theatre); *Soldiers* (Finborough Theatre); *A Midsummer Night's Dream* (RSC/London Sinfonia); *The Lieutenant of Inishmore* (Garrick Theatre); *The Prisoner's Dilemma* (RSC) and *The Iceman Cometh* (Almeida at The Old Vic). Film credits include *The Obelus Evanescence* (T & A Films); *Dear Wendy* (Zentropia); *Vanity Fair* (Universal); *Gangs of New York* (Miramax) and *The Emperor's New Clothes* (Napoleon Films). Television

credits include *Foyles War, Rose and Maloney* (ITV); *Eroica, Down to Earth* (BBC); *Fortysomething* (Carlton); *Peterloo* (Channel 4) and *Longitude* (Granada Films/Channel 4).

Mark Hadfield *Chalky*

Mark's recent theatre credits include *Child of the Snow, Two's Company, Don Juan, Man and Superman, The Lion King*. Other credits include *Cracked, By Many Wounds, The Danube, Amphytrion, Romeo and Juliet, The Taming of the Shrew, The Miser, Blockheads, Becket, Much Ado About Nothing, Guys and Dolls, The Plough and the Stars*, and *Peter Pan*. For the RSC, *Twelfth Night, The Plantaganets* (Barbican); *The Plain Dealer, Bartholomew Fair, Two Gentleman of Verona, The Talk of the City, The Seagull, Jubilee* (Swan); *Kissing The Pope* (Almeida); *The Comedy of Errors/Hamlet* (regional tour); *The Winter's Tale* (World Tour). For the RNT, *Le Bourgeois Gentilhomme* (Lytletton); and *A Midsummer Night's Dream* (Olivier). Film credits, *Tristram Shandy, Felicia's Journey, In the Bleak Midwinter, Mary Shelley's Frankenstein, Just Like a Woman* and *Century*. Television credits include *People Like Us, Casualty, Holby City, Pigsty, Rhona, Posh Nosh, The Wyvern Mystery, The Vice, Cracker, Van Der Valk*, and *Headless*.

David Hounslow *Paul*

David's theatre credits include *Our Boys* (Cockpit Theatre); *The Snowman* (Leicester Haymarket); *Othello* (RSC); *Bent*, *Fuente Ovejuna* (National Theatre); *Treasure Island* (Farnham Redgrave); *Billy Budd* (Crucible, Sheffield); *All of you Mine* (Bush Theatre); *Perpetua*, *My Night with Reg*, *Dealer's Choice* (Birmingham Rep); *Tales from Hollywood*, *Privates on Parade* (Donmar Warehouse); *Holes in the Skin* (Chichester Festival Theatre) and *The Rise and Fall of Little Voice* (Manchester Royal Exchange). Film credits include *Tabloid TV* (Tabloid Productions); *I Want You* (Revolution Films); *The Man Who Knew Too Little* (Warner); *Fever Pitch* (Wildgaze Films) and *Film Captives* (Prisoner Film Productions/BBC). Television credits include *The Brief*, *Heartbeat* (Granada); *The Bill* (Thames); *Holby City*, *Blackpool*, *Crisis Command*, *Eastenders*, *Casualty*, *Silent Witness* (BBC); *Marjorie and Gladys*, *Peak Practice* (Carlton); *London's Burning* (LWT); *North Square* (Lawzone); *Ultimate Force* (Bentley Productions) and *Othello* (BBC/Worldwide).

Neil Stuke *Carl Crassma*

Neil's theatre credits include *Blue/Orange* (Duchess Theatre); *Entertaining Mr Sloane* (Arts Theatre); *Threesome* (Lyric Hammersmith); *The Bullet* (Donmar Warehouse); *Featuring Loretta* (Hampstead Theatre); *Grace Note* (Old Vic); *American Buffalo* (Young Vic); *Mojo* (Duke of Yorks); *Clocks and Whistles*, *Goldhawk Road* (Bush Theatre); *Not a Game for the Boys* (Royal Court); *What the Butler Saw*, *Drinking in America*, *View from the Bridge* and *Romeo and Juliet* (Royal Exchange). Film credits include *Sliding Doors* (Paramount Pictures); *Out on a Limb* (Theta Films); *School for Seduction* (Ipso Facto); *Christy Malry's Own Double Entry* (Kassander Productions); *Circus* (Columbia Pictures); *The Suicide Club* (Concorde Productions); *Mad Cows* (Flashlight Films); *If Only* (Pathe) and *Century* (Breakheart). Television credits include *The Hitch*, *20,000 Streets Under the Sky*, *Bedtime*, *Murder in Mind*, *The Sins*, *Silent Witness* (BBC); *Faith* (Company Pictures); *Murphy's Law* (Tiger Aspect); *Trust* (Box TV); *Grafters* (Granada) and *Game On* (Hat Trick).

Company

Abigail Morris *Director*

Abigail Morris has been Artistic Director of Soho Theatre since 1992. Productions include *Colder Than Here*, *Protection*, *Wrong Place*, *Things You Shouldn't Say Past Midnight*, *Office* (also at Edinburgh International Festival); *Kiss Me Like You Mean It*, *Navy Pier*, *The Station*, *Be My Baby* (at Soho Theatre/national tour); *Waking*, *Tulip Futures*, *The Rock Station* and *Kindertransport* (at the Cockpit, West End and Manhattan Theatre Club, New York). Additional credits include founder of Trouble and Strife Theatre Company, where her productions included the award winning plays *Present Continuous*, *Now and at the*

Hour of Our Death, *Next to You I Lie* (co-writer and director) and various operas including Britten's *Noye's Fludde* (Royal Albert Hall and Festival Hall); *Julius Caesar Jones* (Sadler's Wells) and Cole Porter's *Leave it to Me* (Arts Theatre, Cambridge).

Michael Vale *Designer*

Michael's designs for theatre include *Macbeth* (RSC and tour); *Blues in the Night* (West Yorkshire Playhouse); *Bent* (RNT, West End and tour); *Hedda Gabler* (Manchester Royal Exchange); *Ghosts* (Plymouth Theatre Royal); *Blues for Mr Charlie* (Crucible, Sheffield); *Wind in the Willows* (Bristol Old Vic); *Kidnapped* (Edinburgh Lyceum); *The Three Sisters*, *The White Devil* and *Romeo and Juliet* (Mercury Theatre, Colchester). His designs for opera include *Carmen* and *La Boheme* (Glyndebourne Festival Opera, BBC and Channel 4); *Rigoletto* (ROH, BBC and Olivier Award Nomination); *Tosca* and *Alcina* (ENO and Olivier Award Nomination); *Hamlet* and *Sweeney Todd* (Opera North); *Fidelio* (New Zealand International Festival of The Arts, Wellington); *Idomeneo* (Antwerp De Vlaamse and Los Angeles Opera); *Ariodante* and *The Turn of the Shrew* (Dublin Opera Touring Company, English Touring Opera and Irish Times Theatre Award Nomination). Credits for design and direction include *Doorman* (Plymouth Theatre Royal); *The White Crow* (Colchester Mercury Theatre); *California Suite* (Chester Gateway); *'Art'* and *A Place with the Pigs* (Globe Theatre Company Warsaw) and *They Shoot Cowboys...don't they?* (Edinburgh Pleasance).

Ben Ormerod *Lighting Designer*

Ben's theatre credits include *Head/Case* (Soho Theatre); *Rose Rage* (Brooklyn Academy/Chicago/West End/tour/Watermill); *A Midsummer Night's Dream* (Brooklyn/West End/tour/Watermill); *Macbeth* (West End); *The Constant Wife* (West End/tour); *The Marquise*, *The Circle* (no 1 tours); *Remembrance of Things Past*, *Uncle Vanya*, *Bent*, *Accidental Death of an Anarchist* and *The Winter's Tale* (National Theatre); *John Gabriel Borkmann* (ETT); *The Father* (Athens) and *The Beauty Queen of Leenane* (Broadway/Sydney/Toronto/West End/Druid Theatre). Theatre credits for the RSC include *The Dog in a Manger*, *Tamar's Revenge*, *House of Desire*, *Pedro de Urdemalas*, *Julius Caesar*, *Henry V*, *The Two Gentleman of Verona* and *The Revenger's Tragedy*. Ballet credits include *See Blue Through* (Phoenix Dance Company and Ballet Gulbenkian); *Tender Hooks* (Ballet Gulbenkian); *I Remember Red* (Cullberg Ballet); *A Streetcar Named Desire* (NBT); *Ibi l'ohun* (Brest) and *God's Plenty* (Rambert). Opera credits include *Baa Baa Black Sheep* (Opera North); *Coronation of Poppea* (Japan); *Punch and Judy* (Aldeburgh, Berlin and Vienna) and *Il Trovatore* (Scottish Opera).

Kay Basson *Sound Designer*

Kay's sound design credits include *Who's Afraid of the Big Bad Book* (Soho Theatre); *Aladdin* (Guildford); *Shirley Valentine* (Derby Playhouse); *Forgotten Voices of the Great War* (Pleasance, London); *When the World was Green, Beauty Sleeps* (Young Vic); *Grandads Big Adventure, In Celebration, Secret Rapture, Stairs to the Roof, The Misanthrope, Up on the Roof, Blunt Speaking, The Lady's Not for Burning* (Minerva, Chichester); *Neville's Island, A Christmas Carol, Deadly Manoeuvres, Hiawatha, Pump Boys and Dinettes, Perfect Days, Jungle Book, Marie* and *The Crime Season* (Haymarket, Basingstoke).

Greyhounds UK

All the greyhounds playing Sharkey's Necklace during the run of *A Night at the Dogs* have been involved in the greyhound racing industry and have been lucky enough to find homes once they've retired. Approximately 10,000 dogs retire every year from National Greyhound Racing Club racetracks. The Retired Greyhound Trust found homes for 3110 of the NGRC's retired greyhounds in 2004, but much more needs to be done to address this problem.

I've adopted five retired greyhounds, four of them are only two years old. There are always greyhounds to be found in Battersea Dog's Home, Dog Trust and RSPCA kennels or by ringing the Retired Greyhound Trust on 0870 444 0673.

ANNETTE CROSBIE

Soho Theatre Company would like to thank:

Bell Systems (Telephones) Ltd
Brasserie de Saint-Omer
Redcorn Ltd
Motor Vehicle Dismantlers Association of Great Britain
ReStore Community Projects (Kings Cross Furniture Project)
Western Riverside Authority Refuse

● soho
● theatre + writers' centre

Soho Theatre Company is passionate in its commitment to new writing, producing a year-round programme of bold, original and accessible new plays - many of them from first-time playwrights.

'a foundry for new talent... one of the country's leading producers of new writing'   *Evening Standard*

Soho Theatre + Writers' Centre offers an invaluable resource to emerging playwrights. Our training and outreach programme includes the innovative Under 11s scheme, the Young Writers' Group (15-25s) and a burgeoning series of Nuts and Bolts writing workshops designed to equip new writers with the basic tools of playwriting. We offer the nation's only unsolicited script-reading service, reporting on over 2,000 plays per year. We aim to develop and showcase the most promising new work through the national Verity Bargate Award, the Launch Pad scheme and the Writers' Attachment Programme, working to develop writers not just in theatre but also for TV and film.

a creative hotbed... not only the making of theatre but the cradle for new screenplay and television scripts'   *The Times*

Contemporary, comfortable, air-conditioned and accessible, Soho Theatre is busy from early morning to late at night. Alongside the production of new plays, it is also an intimate venue to see leading national and international comedians in an eclectic programme mixing emerging new talent with established names.

'London's coolest theatre by a mile'   *Midweek*

The Verity Bargate Award

The Award was established in 1982 to honour the memory of Soho Theatre Company's co-founder, Verity Bargate, who set up the Company to discover, develop and produce new plays and new writers. The Award is presented every two years to identify and celebrate the most outstanding unproduced new play by an emerging playwright. Past winners include: Diane Samuels (Kinderstransport), Fraser Grace (Perpetua), Adrian Pagan (The Backroom), Judy Upton (Bruises), Toby Whithouse (Jump Mr Malinoff, Jump) and Shan Khan (Office).

Over 700 entries were received for the Verity Bargate Award 2004 and *A Night at the Dogs* by Matt Charman was announced as the winner at a ceremony on 24 November 2004.

● soho
● theatre + writers' centre

21 Dean St
London W1D 3NE
Admin: 020 7287 5060
Box Office: 0870 429 6883
Minicom: 020 7478 0136
www.sohotheatre.com
email: box@sohotheatre.com

The Terrace Bar

The Terrace Bar serves a range of soft
and alcoholic drinks.

Email information list

For regular programme updates and offers,
join our free email information list by emailing
box@sohotheatre.com
or visiting
www.sohotheatre.com/mailing

Hiring the theatre

Soho Theatre has a range of rooms and spaces
for hire. Please contact the theatre managers on
020 7287 5060
email hires@sohotheatre.com
or go to
www.sohotheatre.com for further details.

Soho Theatre Company

Artistic Director: Abigail Morris
Administrative Producer:
  Mark Godfrey
Associate Director: Jonathan Lloyd
Assistant to Artistic Director:
  Nadine Hoare
Assistant to Administrative
  Producer: Tim Whitehead
Writers' Centre Director:
  Nina Steiger
Literary Assistant: Rachel Taylor
Education and Workshop Officer:
  Suzanne Gorman
Casting Director: Ginny Schiller
Marketing and Development
  Director: Zoe Reed
Development Manager:
  Gayle Rogers
Marketing Officer: Kelly Duffy
Marketing and Development
  Assistant: Zebina Nelson-Myrie
Press Officer: Nancy Poole
  (020 7478 0142)
General Manager:
  Catherine Thornborrow
Front of House and Building
  Manager: Julia Christie
Financial Controller: Kevin Dunn
Book Keeper: Elva Tehan
Box Office Manager: Kate Truefitt
Deputy Box Office Manager:
  Steve Lock
Box Office Assistants: Janice
  Draper, Paula Henstock, Brett
  McCallum, Leah Read, Will
  Sherriff Hammond, Harriet
  Spencer and Natalie Worrall.
Duty Managers : Dominic Delargy,
  Mike Owen, Miranda Yates
  and Peter Youthed.
Front of House staff: Louise
  Beere, Frank Carson, Indi
  Davies, Colin Goodwin, Minho
  Kwon, Ian Marshall, Katherine
  Smith, Rachel Southern, Maya
  Symeou, Ashley Vallance and
  Annabel Wood.

Production Manager:
  Nick Ferguson
Chief Technician: Nick Blount
Chief LX: Christoph Wagner
Lighting Technician: Mark Watts

Board of Directors (*) and Members of the Company

Nicholas Allott*
David Aukin – chair*
Lisa Bryer
Tony Buckley
Sophie Clarke-Jervoise*
Cllr Robert Davis
Barbara Follett MP
Norma Heyman*
Bruce Hyman
Roger Jospé*
Lynne Kirwin
Tony Marchant
Michael Naughton*
David Pelham*
Michael Pennington
Sue Robertson*
Philippe Sands
Eric H Senat
Simon Singh*
Meera Syal
Marc Vlessing*
Zoë Wanamaker
Sir Douglas Wass
Richard Wilson OBE
Roger Wingate*

Honorary Patrons

Bob Hoskins *president*
Peter Brook CBE
Simon Callow
Sir Richard Eyre

The Soho Theatre Development Campaign

Soho Theatre Company receives core funding from Arts Council England, London. In order to provide as diverse a programme as possible and expand our audience development and outreach work, we rely upon additional support from trusts, foundations, individuals and businesses.

All our major sponsors share a common commitment to developing new areas of activity and encouraging creative partnerships between business and the arts.

We are immensely grateful for the invaluable support from our sponsors and patrons and wish to thank them for their continued commitment.

Soho Theatre Company has a Friends Scheme to support its education programme and work in developing new writers and reaching new audiences. To find out how to become a Friend of Soho Theatre, contact the development department on 020 7478 0111, email development@sohotheatre.com or visit www.sohotheatre.com

Sponsors   American Express • Angels, the costumiers • Arts & Business • Getty Images • Tequila\London

Major Supporters and Education Patrons   Tony and Rita Gallagher • Nigel Gee • Roger Jospé • Jack and Linda Keenan • The Regent Street Association • The Garfield Weston Foundation • The Harold Hyam Wingate Foundation

Trusts and Foundations   Anonymous • The Ernest Cook Trust • The Delfont Foundation • Leopold de Rothschild Charitable Trust • The Follett Trust • JG Hogg Charitable Trust • Hyde Park Place Estate Charity • John Lewis, Oxford Street • The Kobler Trust • Linbury Trust • The Mackintosh Foundation • The Royal Victoria Hall Foundation • The St James's Trust • The Edward and Lois Sieff Charitable Trust • Unity Theatre Trust • The Hazel Wood Charitable Trust

Dear Friends   Anonymous • Jill and Michael Barrington • Jos Chambers • David Day • John Drummond • Madeleine Hamel • SoFie and Le'le' • Michael and Mimi Naughton • Oberon Books • Robert Paddick, Commonwealth Partners Ltd • Rick Russell, Final Cut Ltd • Richard and Diana Toeman • Jan and Michael Topham • Carolyn Ward • Piper Smith Watton

Friends   Thank you also to the many Soho Friends we are unable to list here. For a full list of our patrons, please visit www.sohotheatre.com

Registered Charity: 267234

A Night at the Dogs
Matt Charman

faber and faber

First published in 2005
by Faber and Faber Limited
3 Queen Square London WC1N 3AU

Typeset by Country Setting, Kingsdown, Kent CT14 8ES
Printed in England by Mackays of Chatham plc, Chatham, Kent

A CIP record for this book
is available from the British Library

ISBN 0-571-22933-6

2 4 6 8 10 9 7 5 3 1

Characters

Carl
late thirties

Danny
mid-twenties

Chalky
early forties

Lionel
early fifties

Paul
mid-forties

Setting

A one-bedroomed flat in the South of England.

Act One
Carl's lounge and kitchen. Early evening.

Act Two
Carl's bedroom. Later that evening.

A NIGHT AT THE DOGS

For Edward, Anwen and my family,
and with thanks to Nina Steiger
and everyone at the Soho Theatre
for pulling out all the stops

Act One

A sparse one-bedroomed flat. It is completely dark except for one naked bulb lighting a raised kitchenette at the rear. Inside the kitchenette is a tiny table at which Carl sits opposite his younger brother Danny. They are towards the end of their evening meal.

Danny has given up on his dinner and has a burning cigarette in his hand. Carl is still eating. We hear the sounds of an estate and the light hum of traffic outside.

Danny is watching his brother eat and trying to read his expression. It is important to him that Carl is enjoying the food. Neither man speaks. Danny smokes nervously and waits.

Carl finally clears his plate and puts his fork down. He sits back and exhales.

Danny Well?

Carl Well, I'm not convinced, to be honest with you, Danny.

Pause. Danny looks disappointed and taps his cigarette on the edge of the ashtray. He stands.

Danny Fine. (*Quietly he begins clearing away the dishes.*)

Carl Don't get me wrong, I appreciate the gesture of you cooking and all that.

Danny You don't have to say any more.

Carl Well, they don't go very far, do they? Vegetables I mean. They don't stretch very far to filling you up. (*Beat.*) Which even you've got to admit is a pretty big weakness.

Danny You don't have to be full after every meal. It isn't right to be stuffed full.

Carl But would it hurt, Danny, just to have a little bit of meat with this kind of a meal to, you know, fill a gap? Take the edge off, hunger-wise. (*Beat.*) Danny?

Danny I just fancied a change, that's all. We don't have to talk about it any more.

Carl A balanced diet, that's all I'm asking for.

Danny (*uneasy*) Okay.

Carl Okay.

> *Pause.*
> *Still standing, Danny stubs out his cigarette and tucks in his chair. He looks like he is ready to leave.*

Danny So . . .

Carl So what's the big hurry?

Danny I'm going.

Carl You're always going lately. You're always heading off somewhere. Thursday-night dinner with your brother is sacred. Sacred. Where are you going?

> *Danny hesitates.*

Danny Nowhere. Back to my place and then out.

Carl Nowhere? That's two places. Danny? (*Beat.*) Daniel?

Danny I know it is.

Carl I had hoped you might change your plans for tonight. Danny? (*Beat.*) Daniel?

Danny I'm going out tonight.

Carl (*beat*) It's not just what the meal tastes like, of course. It's the presentation. Did you notice that it's practically all white? Everything on the plate. Potatoes, rice, cauliflower. (*Pause.*) Everyone's expecting you to be here. It's important to me.

Danny I won't be here.

Carl I need you to be here.

Danny You'll be fine.

Carl I know I'll be fine. (*Beat.*) I expect you're wishing you'd taken a share in this syndicate. It's fair enough.

Danny You offered me a share. I didn't want it.

Carl I'm offering again.

Danny I can't afford it.

Carl You can afford it.

Danny I can't. I'm saving. Besides, you've got four people, you've got a full syndicate, you'll be fine.

Carl (*disappointed*) I know we'll be fine. (*Beat.*) So what is it?

Danny What?

Carl That you're saving for?

Danny For things.

Carl In particular?

Danny For things that I'm saving for.

Carl For something in particular, though?

Danny Of course for something.

Carl (*beat*) You can afford a stake.

Danny (*frustrated*) I told you, I'm saving.

9

Carl For what, though?

Danny I'm getting married.

Carl is shocked, and for a moment they just look at one another.

We've been engaged for two months. I'm seeing her tonight, I'm saving up . . .

This lingers in the silence.

Carl People need some colour on their plate, Danny, not a plate full of white.

Danny Did you hear what I said?

Carl (*beat*) Do you have a date in mind?

Danny Not yet. Autumn maybe. Look, I didn't tell you because –

Carl (*with force*) I know you didn't tell me, because I'm hearing it for the first time now, while I'm digesting this shit and trying to relax in my own home.

Danny looks down.
Pause. Carl seems hurt.

Danny I just think you've got to take better care of yourself – I might not be around here so much now, you know.

Pause.

Carl Who is she?

Danny Mellinda.

Carl (*beat*) With the clicky hips?

Danny With the what?

Carl What's her surname?

Danny Her surname?

Carl From the shops, isn't she from the corner shops? The mini-market? What's her name? Mellinda . . .

Danny Mellinda –

Carl Don't tell me, I know it. I ought to know it. Mellinda . . . Mellinda . . . Mellinda Handley!

Danny Mellinda Stanley.

Carl Right. With the clicky hips.

Danny What the bloody hell does that mean – clicky hips?

Carl She was born with bad hips. They click. You must have heard them.

Danny Her hips?

Carl Yeah. When she's packing shelves or walking down the aisles in there, they click.

Danny And that's the first thing you notice about her? Not her face, not her beautiful face?

Carl Is she beautiful?

Danny She's gorgeous, you said so.

Carl I can't remember. I did have a conversation with her dad, though, I remember that. When she was born. 'Complications at birth,' he said. I said, 'Really, what with?' 'Clicky hips,' he said.

Danny (*standing*) That's bullshit and that is not a medical term.

Carl Maybe not but they certainly do – click!

Danny (*having worked it out*) You'd have to have been eight when you had that conversation. You're only eight years older than her now. Her father would have been talking about the birth of his new baby girl to an eight-year-old.

Carl Maybe so, Danny. Maybe so. Listen out for them. (*Pause.*) Is it serious between the two of you?

Danny We're engaged.

Carl It's a serious engagement is it? I mean –

Danny shakes his head and makes a move.

Danny I'm going.

Carl Don't go. Don't go like that. I'm asking some questions. I'm two months behind the times here.

Danny It's a secret engagement.

Carl Why?

Danny She's worried about telling her dad.

Carl About you? Why? What's the matter with you?

Danny He's protective. Very protective.

Carl Father's always are over sick kids.

Danny What?

Carl Kids that aren't right – no, let me put it another way. (*slowly spelling it out*) Fathers are always protective over special kids.

Danny She does not have clicky hips, whatever the hell they are.

Carl A legacy, an absolute legacy of medical problems with that one. Years of trouble. Clicking now . . .

Danny That's it.

Danny walks through to the lounge and switches on a small lamp on the sideboard. He looks around for his coat, which he locates on the other side of the room.

Carl What about in five years? Ten years? She'll be leaning on you like an old woman before she's forty.

Danny (*rummaging through his pockets*) This is why I don't say anything. This is exactly the reason why . . .

Danny pulls out a photo from his wallet and steps back into the kitchen.

There. Look at her face and tell me the first thing that springs into your mind is clicky hips.

Carl takes the photo and studies it for a moment.

Carl (*nods*) I'm not disputing the looks aspect, Danny, but what about kids?

Danny We just got engaged.

Carl Do you pass it on, though? That sort of condition, is it – ?

Danny (*takes the photograph back*) Genetic?

Carl That would be my fear.

He lights up a cigarette. Danny hovers.

Are you not going then?

Danny (*pause*) I never heard them make a noise . . .

Carl offers him a cigarette. He shakes his head.

No, I quit, she doesn't like it.

Carl You were just smoking. I saw you.

Danny I just quit, just now. That was my last.

Carl takes a long puff.

Can you honestly hear them?

Carl Yes, but I'm not the best judge. My hearing is really very good. Ask someone else. Rick's coming. Ask Rick if he's heard them.

Danny Don't say a word to anyone.

Carl laughs.

Oh, fuck off.

Carl (*smiles again*) Alright, alright.

Danny (*beat*) I'm serious now.

Carl You're not gonna be moody for the rest of the night, are you? Please, Dan, I couldn't bear it. You know how important tonight is for me, don't spoil it with a mood. Stay for one drink? One drink is all.

No response.

(*angry*) For fuck sake at least have one drink? It's a big night.

Danny For both of us. You've got this syndicate – it's your syndicate, you've got this dog. I'm pleased for you, but I've got something else now. Can't you just be pleased for me?

Carl You should be here.

Danny Look, we're telling her dad tonight but I wanted to tell you first. I wanted to cook you a good meal and tell you. I'm sorry it didn't come out right but I want you to be happy about this, it's important to me. She'll be your sister-in-law.

Carl I hardly know her.

Danny You'll get to know her.

Pause.

Carl I suppose you don't notice the clicking after a while.

Danny Right, fuck off.

Carl laughs.

This is why I don't say anything – this is exactly why I leave telling you to the last possible moment.

Danny picks up the plates and takes them to the kitchen.

Carl Do you want my blessing, Danny boy? Is that it? I'll tell you, for what it's worth. Are you listening? Women! They're all fucking mad. That's it, Daniel, in a nutshell – no charge.

> *The door buzzer goes.*
> *Carl gets up excitedly and steps over to the intercom, which he presses and speaks into.*

Who is it?

> *We hear a fuzzy reply through the speaker before Carl presses the door-release catch and steps back.*

It's Chalky.

Danny Fine. (*Pause.*) I've got to go anyway. (*Searching for his coat, which he locates.*)

Carl Don't go. Stay and have a drink with Chalky.

Danny I just spent all day with him. I want to go.

> *Carl ignores this.*
> *There is a knock at the door, which Danny opens with his jacket in his hand ready to leave. Chalky walks in with a playful grin and his hands in his coat pockets.*

Chalky Reeks of piss all up that hallway.

Carl It's disinfectant.

Chalky Well, it smells like piss. I'm not bothered, I'm just saying. (*Beat.*) Alright, Dan?

Danny Alright, Chalky?

Chalky Are you coming down the track?

Danny (*anxious but amiable*) No, I can't – I'm on my way out, Chalk.

Carl winks and offers Chalky a seat.

Carl He's staying for one drink. Drink, Chalky?

Chalky Bottle of – if you've got one.

Chalky sits and unzips his jacket.

Carl Daniel, get Mr Chalk a bottle of lager will you?

Carl and Danny exchange stares. Carl wins and Danny slams the door, throwing his jacket on a chair as he stalks through into the kitchen, towards the fridge.
Pause.

Chalky I'm fired up. About tonight, you know, I'm excited. I've been thinking about it all day.

Carl That's good.

Chalky Yeah, I know. I'm saying I'm looking forward to it . . .

Danny passes Chalky and Carl a bottle of beer.

Cheers . . .

They raise them to one another and take a drink.
Pause.

This wicker's uncomfortable.

Carl Well, you're sitting in it wrong. You're slouching. You don't slouch in wicker.

Chalky It cuts the circulation off in your legs.

Carl When you're slouching, maybe.

Chalky (*looking around*) Is it garden furniture? Is that it?

Carl It's a chair, Chalky. It's a wicker chair.

Chalky Danny, is this garden furniture?

Danny Sit somewhere else, Chalky.

Chalky (*sitting upright*) I'm not bothered, I'm just saying.

   Pause. Danny shifts about from foot to foot.

Danny (*breaking the awkward silence*) First race, then, for the syndicate.

Carl It's her debut, that's what they call it. I mean, she's raced before.

Chalky She hasn't won before, mind you.

Carl (*put out*) Well, she's been in training. This is a sport, Chalky, like any other. It's all discipline and breeding and attention to detail. I mean, you've got to train the bloody dog.

Chalky I know, but I'm saying, she hasn't won a training race yet.

Carl (*unconvincing*) Yes, she has.

Chalky Has she?

Carl (*equally unconvincing*) Of course.

Danny (*slowly and smiling*) Has she?

   Carl takes a strategic sip to buy himself some time before carrying on.

Carl Round the yard where they train her, they have races. She wins all the time.

Chalky (*pleased with this answer*) I like the sound of that.

   Danny stares at Carl, who feels his gaze and goes on to justify himself. He nods and takes a drink.

Carl They're not what you'd call full-distance races. They're just little sprints, but she's been winning them all . . . some of them.

Chalky She's quick alright.

Carl I don't know a faster dog.

Danny (*laughs*) You can't say that! Be realistic at least.

Carl Up and coming, I mean. (*pissed off*) You don't know what you're talking about. I'm a realist and I also happen to know what I'm talking about.

   Danny laughs again.

Chalky No, fair's fair, Dan. Your brother's an aficionado of the track.

Danny Is that what they call it?

Chalky He studies form, weight, finishes, blood types . . .

Danny Blood types?

Carl Breeding, he means breeding.

Chalky That's right, breeding. Then there's whether they were crowded at the start, bumped at a corner, all that stuff – expert.

Carl She's an investment.

Chalky Three hundred quid each splits the dog four ways. Me, Carl, Lionel and Rick. (*to himself*) That's a leg each. (*to Danny*) As they say in the business.

Carl That covers the dog, the kennel, the special diet, all that stuff. That's an outlay that is. When you invest in something you better know what you're investing in, or you end up losing your shirt.

Chalky Here's to a sound investment.

They toast again and take a drink. Danny puts on his jacket.

You might live to regret not joining this little syndicate of ours, Danny.

Danny Could be. (*Beat.*) Right!

Carl What?

Danny I'm off now.

Chalky He's off now. (*He stands.*) Alright, Danny, good seeing you. (*Offers a hand.*)

Carl Sit down. He's not going anywhere.

Chalky Oh? (*He sits.*)

Danny Carl!

Carl Will you buck up or fuck off, Danny!

Danny I'm trying to leave!

Carl Stay and finish your drink, for pity's sake! I told Rick you'd be here.

> *Pause.*
> *Chalky sips his beer.*
> *Danny glances at his watch.*
> *Carl looks around, trying to think up conversation.*

Carl Crisps?

Chalky Got any?

Carl No.

Chalky I'm alright. I'll eat at the track.

Carl Oh, there'll be food at the track.

Chalky I know.

> *Beat. Chalky laughs.*

Carl What?

Chalky No, nothing, I was just . . . (*Laughs.*) What's that tune again?

Carl What tune?

Chalky That tune he sings. (*Laughs.*)

Danny Rick?

Chalky He's been singing this thing, and he changes the words and puts my name into the song. (*laughing*) It's really very clever, he's very quick. He keeps doing it. What is it lately?

Danny (*half-singing to the Dean Martin tune*)
'When Chalky's smiling . . .'

Chalky That's it.

Danny *and* **Chalky** (*half-singing*)
'When Chalky's smiling.
The whole world smiles with Chalk.
And when Chalky's dancing . . .'

Carl Bloody hell.

Chalky 'When he's dancing.' (*almost nostalgic*) That's beautiful. He's so quick with it.

Carl Chalky, please!

Chalky What?

Carl It's very annoying, you know. Especially when I really need to concentrate tonight – get my head straight.

Chalky Of course, sorry, Carl.

The door-buzzer sounds. Carl steps over to it.

Carl (*in a poor Spanish accent, speaking into the intercom*) Carlos the Jackal's residence!

Chalky That doesn't work, they caught him. (*Pleased with himself.*) Dan, I said that doesn't work any more.

Danny I heard you, Chalky, you're right, it doesn't.

Carl Shut up, Chalky. (*He presses the buzzer.*) Come on up. (*He fumbles with the switch.*) Try pressing it now!

    Pause.

Chalky (*looking around*) You haven't decorated then?

Carl I've done bits and pieces here and there.

Chalky Here and where?

Carl I've only just moved my stuff in, Chalky.

Chalky You've been here six months.

Carl And already the bathroom's practically good as new.

Chalky (*goes to stand*) Oh, well, I'll take a look.

Carl Sit down. (*Beat.*) I mean it's coming on. It's halfway there. Don't get up.

Danny He hasn't started it.

Carl Shut up. I take my time. Do it right. I could bolt round in a weekend and get stuff done, but would it last?

Chalky I don't know, would it?

    Lionel wanders in. He is a big man and miserable-looking. The door shuts.

Carl Alright, then?

Chalky Alright, Lionel?

Danny Drink, Lionel?

Lionel (*sitting down*) Not beer.

Carl Not beer, right you are.

Lionel Smells of piss in that hallway.

Chalky I agree.

Lionel Cat's piss.

Carl It's disinfectant.

Lionel Smells like cat's piss to me. Any Scotch?

Carl (*peering into the drinks cupboard*) It's bad for you. I don't keep it in the house.

Lionel Bad for who?

Carl Bad for you, for everyone, all of us. Bad for the liver. Too severe.

Lionel Too expensive!

Carl (*affecting a deeply hurt tone*) If you don't mind, Lionel, we had an uncle who died of cirrhosis of the liver. Alright? Brought about, in most part, because of his love of Scotch.

Danny And vodka . . . and gin . . . and meths . . .

They all laugh except Carl.

Carl Oh sure, alcoholism is fucking hilarious.

Chalky Sorry, Carl.

Carl (*still pissed off*) Lionel – I've got Tia Maria. Drink as much as you like, it was Carole's.

Lionel (*flatly*) Fine. Great. I don't care. Just not beer, it bloats me up.

Carl pours it and brings it over to Lionel. He stands expectantly while Lionel sips and realises he is supposed to comment.

Lionel Oh right – sorry, very nice.

They sit in silence. Danny looks around, thoroughly bored. Chalky glances at his watch.

Pause.

Chalky What time is she –

Carl Nine, we've got plenty of time to get her to the track.

The silence envelopes them again. Chalky smiles.

Chalky (*lightly under his breath*) 'When Chalky's dancing . . .'

This is met with a stony stare from Carl, and as the line dies, Chalky's smile fades.
Pause.
Danny looks at his beer bottle, necks it and makes to leave.

Danny Right then.

Carl (*desperately*) Danny's got himself engaged.

There is a murmur of congratulations from Lionel and Chalky.

Danny Hold on –

Carl Dan, I'm sorry. Fellas listen – it's not official yet.

Danny No, it bloody isn't. Jesus!

Carl No, that's my mistake. Hands up to that one. I'm obviously very proud and it popped out and I shouldn't have said a word. Not a word, lads, please, to anyone.

Danny Please!?

Chalky And who am I gonna tell? I work all day with you lot.

Lionel Who is she?

Chalky Mellinda from the mini-market.

Danny Bloody hell!

Lionel Oh right, I know her, clicky hips.

Danny Will you shut up about her fucking hips. And how the hell do you know, Chalky?

Chalky Well, you've been seeing her for a while now, haven't you?

Danny Yeah . . . I –

Chalky I mean, who else is it going to be?

Danny Well, no one, but . . .

Chalky Don't be angry, Dan. It's nice.

Carl Show them the photo then!

> *Danny reluctantly takes out the photograph and shows it to Lionel and Chalky, who lean in.*

And . . .?

Chalky Lovely!

Lionel Lovely skin. (*Beat.*) Is she a goer, then, or –

> *Danny withdraws the photograph.*

Danny Don't be disgusting, Lionel.

Carl Yeah, Alright, come on, break it up – she's Dan's girl.

> *Pause.*
> *They drink in silence.*

Lionel (*slowly, as if this is troubling him*) We had a little sports car come in today that had come round a corner too fast and hit a horse.

Carl We know.

Lionel A little sports car it was, with a soft top and alloy wheels.

Carl We saw it, Lionel. We all came out and had a look at it.

Lionel Did you?

Carl (*tutting*) Did we!? Don't you remember?

Chalky It was a Mazda.

Carl It was a fucking Toyota Celica, the new shape.

Chalky Was it, Dan?

Carl Dan . . . ?

Danny (*out of loyalty*) It was a Toyota, Chalky.

Lionel It was a right state. Blood and flesh, looked like liver, uncooked liver all over the windscreen and on the leather seats.

Carl Right mess.

Lionel Blood on the seats.

Danny Really?

Carl It was a soft-top, so this horse must have ended up practically in the driver's lap. Terrible state, blood, flesh!

Chalky (*to himself*) You can eat horse.

Carl Not this one – fucking state. Must have killed the animal. On a bend, country lane. Imagine that. Imagine hitting a fucking horse coming round a bend on a country lane.

Chalky I hit an old woman once.

They all turn and look at Chalky as they take this in.

Danny What's that, Chalky?

Chalky At a junction. I looked one way, then the next, and she stepped off the kerb and I hit her, gently. Sort of brushed her.

Lionel With a car?

Chalky But not hard, you know. No speed at all.

Danny Was she hurt?

Carl He hit her with a fucking car, of course she was hurt.

Chalky (*defensively*) No, nothing was broken or ruptured or . . . she wasn't in pain at all. I stayed with her.

Lionel (*pause*) Did you call an ambulance, then?

Chalky This was before mobile phones, this was years ago. I was your age, Dan. No, I couldn't call anybody, I just parked up, moved her off the road and stayed with her. She got up after about twenty minutes and carried on walking into town. I offered her a lift, but . . . Still . . . (*This hangs in the air.*)

Danny Still what?

Chalky I felt bad.

Carl Well, you would. You would feel bad. That was somebody's . . . you know, mother, or whatever. You could have killed her.

Chalky I didn't kill her.

Danny Carl, leave him alone.

Carl No, I'm not getting at you, Chalky, but you had good reason to feel bad. (*Beat.*) Negligent – what's the word? . . . (*He considers.*) I'll stick with negligent.

26

Pause. Chalky thinks for a moment.

Chalky (*worried*) I never thought about it as somebody's mother. It might not have been anybody's mother, you know – she might not have had children.

Carl Well, if she didn't then, she probably wouldn't be able to now – knocks like that can affect a woman – womb-wise.

Chalky She was a pensioner, what would she want with kids?

Danny Take no notice, Chalky. (*to Carl*) For pity's sake, it was years ago.

Carl (*sarcastic*) Alright! Alright! I think it's perfectly fine that you knocked an old woman down, Chalky. I have no problem with it. You didn't call an ambulance, but you sat with her so that's practically the same, what with your extensive medical training . . .

Danny That's enough, now.

Pause.

Lionel So was the driver killed, then? I mean, did the horse kill him going through the windscreen?

Carl I don't know, Lionel. I don't know the history of the situation. We're a crash-and-repair outfit. Car comes in, you two rebuild it. (*Points to Chalky.*) He paints it and I valet it.

Chalky (*stifling a laugh*) Valet it!

Carl What?

Lionel Wash. Surely the word is wash.

The men laugh a little.

Carl Eleven different types of fluid I use on a car.

Danny (*light-hearted*) No, no – I can't hear this again.

Chalky (*smiling*) Yes, again!

Carl (*enjoying this*) That's not a fucking wash, my friend, that's a four –

Danny echoes his words.

– wheeled miracle when I've finished with it.

The men laugh.

Chalky He's good, give him credit where it's due.

Carl Good? I've been washing the boss's Merc for nine years. Three different Mercs in that time and I've washed every one of the fuckers. I know those cars better than he does.

Danny Alright, alright.

Chalky Show them the letter.

Lionel What letter?

Carl I'm not showing anybody that letter.

Chalky Someone wrote him a letter.

Carl There are two letters, actually.

Lionel Love letters?

Carl A letter to me.

Chalky A thank-you letter.

Carl More a letter of – Danny, what's the word?

Danny Commendation.

Carl Yes, yes, that's the word.

Chalky You seen it, Dan?

Danny nods.

Lionel Someone wrote to you, personally?

Chalky Read it out!

Carl I'm not reading it out.

Danny Don't read it out.

Beat.

Carl Alright, I'll read it out . . .

He steps over to the sideboard and picks up a frame.

Lionel You framed it?

Carl (*defensive*) To keep it flat, that's all.

He looks at the letter and then back at them.

Just to keep it flat. (*reading*) 'Dear Sir/Madam, I am writing to express my deepest thanks to you. As you know my car was recently with you for a repair to the offside front. The car was delivered back home on Thursday 4th April. Not only was the repair absolutely perfect, the paintwork is a glass finish. I would also like to praise your cleaning department, my car is spotless inside and out. I know most people only write to complain but I think my insurance company should know how well you are repairing cars for them. Also I would have no compunction in referring anyone wishing to get their car repaired by you. Best regards, Mr David Richardson.'

Chalky Now isn't that a nice letter?

Lionel Is that it?

Danny It's not exactly a letter you frame, is it?

Carl (*placing it back on the sideboard*) What's that?

Chalky It's a nice letter.

Carl There's another one.

Lionel Did you frame that too?

Carl I don't frame every letter of –

Danny Commendation.

Carl – commendation I get, Lionel. If I did I'd have –

Danny Two?

Lionel laughs a little and Danny joins in guiltily.

Carl (*very offended*) Oh, fuck this. (*to Danny*) Anyone ever write to you?

Danny (*still laughing*) Brother, I'm just joking.

Carl Are you? So am I. Anyone ever write to you to say you'd done a good job?

Danny Of course not.

Carl Why of course not? Don't you deserve it, don't you do a good job, don't you deserve a little praise?

Danny I do a job. If I do it wrong, I do it again. If I do it right, I've done my job, you know how it works.

Carl So how do you explain this?

Danny It was a general letter. It was to everybody. It wasn't just about how clean the car was – it's addressed to everybody. I told you that when you framed it. (*He steps back over to the frame and picks it up.*)

Carl 'Spotless inside and out.'

Danny Okay, but it's a general letter in its tone, you know.

Carl (*mocking*) Oh, in its tone. Oh perhaps I'm missing out on its tone, Danny? That must be a secret tone only you can hear, where 'Well done, good job,' means something else altogether.

Danny Forget it.

Carl That's a pretty fucking different tone.

Danny Carl, you're spitting on me. (*Pause.*)

Chalky What does the other one say?

Carl No bloody chance. No way. Not after that reaction. For my eyes only.

Carl returns the frame to the sideboard. The men drink in silence.
  Chalky nods at Danny, who grudgingly offers an apology.

Danny Sorry, brother.

Pause.

Chalky We're just waiting on Rick, then? And the dog.

Carl (*anxious*) Any minute now. Danny's waiting to see her, aren't you, Dan?

Danny Yes.

Carl I told him. I said he'll wanna see the dog, won't he? She'll have the little jacket on that's been made for her. You'll wanna see that, won't you, Dan?

Danny (*flatly*) Yes, Carl.

Lionel Are we going to talk about the name of this greyhound or not?

Carl (*defensively*) Why?

Chalky Well . . .

Carl Well?

Chalky Naming the dog – well, it's an important part of the whole . . .

Lionel Are we set on the name?

Danny What name?

Lionel The dog's name. Your brother chose it.

   Pause. Carl seems embarrassed.

Danny Let's hear it, then.

Carl Sharkey's Necklace. The dog is called Sharkey's Necklace.

   There is a pause. Carl glances at Danny.

Chalky And what is that then?

Lionel Exactly. Everyone asks me that. 'What's that then? Who's Sharkey?'

Chalky People ask me too, Carl.

Lionel You want a name where there's no doubt in anybody's mind. A quick name. A grand name.

Chalky I mean what is Sharkey's Necklace when it's at home?

Lionel Like Rhinestone Cowboy, I've been thinking about that, as a name. (*Beat.*) As in the song.

Chalky (*feeling empowered*) I tend to come up with words, not names, not complete names. (*He gets a piece of paper out of his pocket.*) Ruby. Villain. Eclipse. Champagne. Gandhi.

Danny Gandhi?

Chalky As a suggestion. Broadly speaking.

Carl You can't call a racing dog Gandhi.

Chalky I was casting the net wide.

Danny Mahatma Gandhi?

Chalky Well, he could do no wrong, and he was a skinny little fella just like the dog is skinny and –

Carl A racing animal, a dog people put money down on, and you wanna call it Gandhi?

Chalky It seemed to fit to me. It's just an idea.

Lionel It's a fucking ridiculous idea.

Chalky (*folding up the paper*) So it needs work.

Lionel It really does.

Chalky (*feeling strongly*) At least mine are good words, I think. They feel like the right words. At least people know what they mean.

Lionel As opposed to –

Danny Sharkey's Necklace.

Carl But that is what the dog is called. It's in the race guide.

Chalky This week. It's in the race guide this week. But that's what we wanted to talk to you about, Carl.

Lionel I think that we should all have been consulted.

Carl You were consulted.

Chalky We were?

Lionel We weren't, Carl.

Carl I said I'm going to need some suggestions for names for the entry form for the race. I said that two weeks ago.

Lionel During a fag break. Next time I asked you'd come up with a name and posted in the form.

Carl The deadline came and went and no one said a word. I'm not wiping arses, Lionel. If I say something once, then it's been said.

Lionel A little reminder wouldn't have hurt, that's all.

Carl No, no – absolutely not. The whole fucking country works on little reminders. Listen the first time when I tell you for the first time. Engage your fucking brain when I tell you something and you won't need a little reminder. Unless you're suggesting I write it down, and let you have it on a fucking Post-It note? If I had my way I'd take all the fucking Post-It notes in the world and build a huge fucking bonfire with them so people had to listen the first time.

Danny (*calming him*) Alright, brother.

Carl Well, have a little bit of grace. You're sitting in my lounge drinking my beer, me having organised the entire evening, not to mention this whole bloody syndicate. The kennel, the money, the injections and all that, all of it, and I get no praise but instead I'm told that I should have given people 'little reminders', when I told them perfectly well the first time.

> *Pause.*
> *Danny gestures to Lionel and Carl that they ought to apologise.*

Lionel Alright.

Chalky Sorry, Carl.

Carl Right, well –

Chalky Perhaps now we know we could change the name . . .

> *The buzzer goes and Carl steps over to it quickly.*

Carl Sit tight, I've got it. (*into the intercom*) Hello? (*He hears the voice and unconsciously changes the way he is standing, becoming more upright.*) Hello, mate, how are you? Coming up? No, it'll be safe enough if you've parked it out by the bins under the lights. Come up. (*He presses the buzzer and picks up the handset.*) I'll open the door. Come up . . . (*A little nervous laughter.*) Oh, he's gone.

Carl goes and opens the door. When he is done, he turns to the men, folds his arms and looks nervously at them.

Danny (*suspicious*) That's not Rick, is it?

Carl (*pause*) No.

Chalky (*stands*) Who's that then, Carl?

Carl It's not Rick.

Carl starts to dart his eyes around to look at the state of the flat. He moves a pile of magazines and papers off a chair and onto the floor.

Danny Who is it then?

Lionel Someone's on the stairs.

All of them are focused on the door and silent for a second. After a moment Paul steps in. He is distant, distracted, like he's somehow found himself at Carl's flat without knowing quite how he got there.

Paul Fellas.

All Paul.

Paul Fucking horrible area to live in.

Carl It is, I know. (*Beat.*) I'm sorry for the piss smell, Paul, in the corridor.

Paul That's alright, Carl. No harm done. I've smelt cat's piss before, no doubt I will smell it again. Shut the door, though, it gets right down in your stomach.

Carl shuts the door. Pause.

Chalky Alright, Paul?

Paul I'm remarkably relaxed, Chalky.

Danny Were you stressed?

Paul Pardon me, Daniel?

Danny Before – were you stressed, before? If you're relaxed now, I mean you must have been . . . stressed.

Paul It has been a stressful day.

Chalky I haven't seen you all week, Paul. Not in the workshop, or around at all. You been ill?

Paul I've had things to do. Personal matters. I had to see my solicitor. You remind me of him, Chalky.

Chalky Do I?

Paul Yeah. He asked a lot of fucking questions as well.

Carl (*slightly nervous, but taking charge*) Quite right. Enough fucking questions. Drink, Paul?

Paul Beer.

Carl (*gesturing towards the kitchen*) Danny, would you get Paul a beer from the kitchen, please?

Danny Well, I was actually heading . . .

Danny sees the look Carl gives him and he trails off.

Right.

Carl Fellas? Drinks?

They shake their heads.
    Paul sits down and looks around. All the men are watching him carefully. Danny brings a beer from the kitchen and passes it to Paul. He takes it and checks the time.

Paul Where's this dog, then?

Carl (*looking at his watch*) Where is this dog, then? Good question. He'll be here, Paul.

Danny You a fan of dog-racing then, Paul?

Paul Not until I bought a stake in one, no.

Danny and Lionel both look at Carl, understanding what this means.

Chalky That's funny, you as well? Everybody's doing it, aren't they? We've got a syndicate together as well, Paul.

They all look at Chalky and the penny drops.

Oh, I see.

Paul (*distracted*) That's right. (*Beat.*) Now I'm a convert. Now I'm reading form guides, now I'm understanding the rules. Now I'm a fan.

Carl That's great, isn't it, fellas?

Paul Where's the toilet? Or do I just go out in the corridor.

He laughs a little and Carl forces a smile.

Carl (*pointing a door behind him*) You'll have to be careful, it's a bit of a state in there, I'm halfway through decorating, you know.

Paul (*standing up*) Halfway? How long you lived here now?

Carl Six months.

Paul (*walking to the toilet*) Six months? You ought to be ashamed of yourself.

Carl (*laughing*) I am, Paul, I am.

He shuts the toilet door and there is silence.
  Pause.

Chalky (*whispering*) Four ways, you said. That's five.

Lionel (*standing*) I'm going.

Carl (*whispering*) Don't be stupid, Lionel.

Danny This is why.

Carl What?

Danny Why you wanted me to stay.

Carl Keep your voice down.

Lionel I spend nine hours a day getting told what to do by that little bastard – this is not how I choose to spend my Thursday nights.

Carl That's different, that's work. Sit down.

Danny Punchy Paul! Are you a fucking idiot?

Carl (*whispering*) Keep your voice down. It's a syndicate, he paid his money.

Chalky (*whispering*) Four ways, you said.

Carl (*whispering*) It doesn't affect anything. It's still our dog, it's a syndicate.

Danny Why? Tell me why? How did he hear about it?

Carl (*shrugs his shoulders weakly*) Well, he must have . . . you know, I mean . . . Look, I really don't know. Look, he's in on it now.

Danny Did you tell him? To impress him? Is that why? What's wrong with you?

Chalky There aren't five legs, there are four. I'm not giving up a leg for him.

Lionel Have my leg, I'm going.

Carl (*whispering*) Lionel! Take a seat – Chalky, have the head.

Chalky (*whispering*) What?

Carl (*whispering*) Go on – take the head. If there are only four legs, you can have the head.

Chalky (*whispering*) I don't want the head. The legs are the part that do the running.

Carl (*whispering*) But the head crosses the line first.

Chalky (*thinks for a moment*) I'll have the head. It doesn't bother me . . .

Lionel Well, it bothers me.

Carl Lionel, it's cheaper with five.

Lionel What?

Carl With four the stake is three hundred quid. With five it's more like – Danny?

Danny It's two hundred and forty, but –

Carl So it's cheaper with five is what it is.

Chalky We've paid all the money now, we don't need him now.

Danny It's too late, Chalky. He opened his mouth to impress Paul and you're stuck with him now. Am I right?

Carl He wanted in, on our syndicate. That means something. Look, Paul's not so bad.

Danny He's a fucking lunatic and you know it. (*whispering*) He broke someone's jaw last year for reversing into 'his' parking space in a multistorey.

Carl Don't exaggerate. (*Beat.*) It was dislocated maybe.

Lionel And he throws dinner plates in restaurants.

Carl Once he threw a plate. Once.

Danny What's he gonna do when the dog doesn't win every time? Whose fault will that be?

Carl It's a quick dog.

Danny You better hope so, brother. What were you thinking? It's Punchy Paul, at his fucking solicitor's again. Ask yourself why?

Chalky Why get him involved at all?

Carl I like the man and it's too late to go back now. Look, he's in on it, but I don't think that it's a bad thing. It's a good thing I think, in fact. (*Beat.*) So he's got a temper . . .

Danny He's got a fucking baseball bat in the boot of his car, is what he's got. I'm going.

Carl Please, Dan. Keep your voice down. He's controllable.

The toilet flushes and the door opens. The men's mouths snap shut. Paul steps out and is wiping his hands.

Paul You've got ducks in your toilet. Little model ducks on the shelf. Wood and ceramic.

Carl My ex-wife's.

Paul Then why hasn't she got them?

Carl She got the kids. I stole them. Brought them here. Like hostages. I break one from time to time.

Paul Makes you feel better, doesn't it? (*He puts the towel back in the toilet and shuts the door.*)

Carl (*looks at Danny*) I suppose . . . for a moment or two.

Paul How many kids have you got, Carl?

Carl Me? Two, Paul. A girl and a boy. Eight and ten.

Paul Same here, only mine are older. Sixteen and eighteen. (*Pause.*) See them much?

Carl My kids? Weekends, every other. I pick them up. They come here. We go out. I've got a little lock-up at the back. I'm doing up a boat, just a little . . . it's a dinghy, you know. They're helping me. They love it. Don't they love it, Danny?

Danny nods, but stays looking at Paul.

Paul (*thinks for a moment*) I couldn't have my kids taken away from me, you know. Not like you have. Not to be told when I can see them and have a watch timing me.

Danny It's not ideal, but it happens.

Paul I wouldn't let it happen, Daniel, that's what I'm saying.

Carl They don't need us, though, do they? I've got a brochure around here somewhere. For family health insurance or something . . . anyway, whatever it is, it says 'Family Health' and alongside it there's a photograph of a woman and two kids. (*Beat.*) 'Family.' (*Pause.*) Not a father in sight.

Chalky Someone's got to take the photo.

Carl (*calmly*) The father is being airbrushed out. We're not needed, except to pay for whatever it says in the brochure and visit maybe once a fortnight.

Paul (*seeming to engage for the first time*) So put up a fucking fight.

Carl You're right, Paul, of course, but –

Paul Kids, Lionel?

Lionel Five.

Paul Five?

Carl Bit of a rabbit is our Lionel.

Lionel My wife loves being pregnant. It's when she's happiest. Four boys, one girl, all smart.

Carl (*trying to make Paul laugh*) Take after their mother, do they?

Lionel Just like their mother, actually. I'm not ashamed. She's the brains, she's the planner. She's got it all mapped out, been saving for years for different things. Got a bedside drawer full of brown envelopes with money in them. She writes on the front of them – 'University' or . . . others I can't remember, I don't go prying. She knows what's what. I'm just happy enough if they've got a normal haircut, a few proper exams and a Saturday job.

Carl Too true.

Paul I got one at university, back for the holidays – and one at hairdressing college.

Carl Well, that's wonderful, isn't it?

Paul My two greatest achievements.

Chalky What about your extension?

Paul I'm serious. (*Pause.*)

Carl Yeah, come on, serious now . . . Good on you, Paul. God knows I've got all that planned for my two. The whole university bit, you know. (*to Paul*) And just to set the record straight – I know what you mean about being away from them, and it isn't exactly natural, but I've always thought it isn't natural for them to be without a mother either. Even though she's the one that, you know, fucked it all up. With a close friend of mine. Behind my back.

Pause.

Lionel I always thought you'd go that way, Dan.

Danny What's that?

Lionel University or college. You're smart enough.

Carl Course he is.

Paul You have to be, my two are smart.

Carl (*drops his voice*) Oh, he's not smart like your two, Paul.

Danny Do you think I can't hear you when you drop your voice? I'm only sitting here. I can still hear you.

Carl (*trying to dig himself out of a hole*) You know what I mean, think of the expense and what you'd be learning and why you'd be learning it. What good would it do *you*, Danny? Besides, every bugger's going now. It's not special now is it? The Mickey Mouse courses they run, Media with the . . . History of Art. It's a joke.

Paul One of mine's doing History of Art.

Carl (*back-pedalling*) History of Art is fine. We'll always need that, it's one of the good ones – but not Sports Science, though, Paul – that's the real let-down of modern education.

Paul Who said anything about Sports Science?

Carl I did, right now. I'm saying we've got a bunch of kids who love football so we have to come up with a qualification that rewards that in some way. Call it Sports Science. Get a load of kids in a room watching football talking about formations and using words like 'mental attitude' and then call it a science. Ridiculous. And GNVQs. You know what they stand for – Generally Not Very Qualified. It's true. What are the three most useless things in the world? The Pope's balls, Lionel's tits and a GNVQ in anything . . .

The men laugh hard, except for Lionel. Carl feels in his element.

It's a fucking disgrace, making up these exams so kids with nothing going for them can have a piece of paper to take into an interview.

He allows himself a little laugh before something occurs to him.

None of yours did a GNVQ did they, Paul?

Paul No.

Carl Of course they didn't.

Danny *(to Carl)* And are you saving, for your two? Got any brown envelopes in the bedside table, brother?

Carl Saving? Yes, of course I am. However, mine is a slightly more advanced system.

Danny Oh really?

Carl As a matter of fact, yes. It's a speculate-to-accumulate system.

Danny *(laughing)* It's not betting on the bloody dog, I hope? *(Stops laughing.)* You are joking?

Carl Yes, the dog, of course. I'll take twenty-five per cent out of everything she wins me and put it to one side.

Chalky In an envelope?

Carl That's not important – the most important thing is, it will be earmarked.

Danny Bloody hell. Do you know how much tuition fees for university are? She better start winning, Carl.

Carl I've got it worked out. She has to win at two meetings a month.

Paul Two? She better win at a damn sight more than two.

Carl (*nervously*) Oh, she will, she will.

Chalky Course she will. I haven't worked out what I'll spend it on. I've been thinking, but I haven't made a decision. Maybe a big bathtub that you can float in.

Danny They call them swimming pools, Chalky.

Carl Then there's the money you get from breeding her, you know – and that's big money with her being a pedigree and sought-after.

Chalky I didn't think of that.

Carl (*smiles*) I have . . . thought of it all, worked it all out.

Danny That's not how you make money out of it though, surely? By betting on your own dog.

Carl (*unsure*) I know, Danny.

Danny But –

Carl (*embarrassed over the uncertainty*) Daniel, I said I know.

> *There is a pause. The men drink. Chalky is uncomfortable with the silence.*

Chalky So what's been going on then, Paul?

Paul Sorry?

Chalky (*panicking*) Nothing.

Carl (*to Paul*) Nothing, pay no attention.

Paul (*to Chalky*) What do you mean by that?

Chalky I mean, you know – was it a bad visit to the solicitor's or a good one?

Paul Have you paid a good visit to the solicitor's lately, Chalky?

Chalky I don't know, I don't really know what I'm talking about. I'm sorry.

Pause.

Paul I was at the solicitor's today because of a crime that someone has committed to my family. To my child.

There is a longish pause. Paul's breathing is slow and noticeable.

Chalky Oh . . .

Pause.

Paul My wife hasn't slept for three nights. I've got her some pills now. I dish them out to her because it's a bad thing to be taking pills and I don't want her doing it behind my back . . . My child has been . . . my own baby has been . . . someone has forced themselves inside my own flesh and blood – like some . . . on the fucking lawn outside my own front door, on a little patch of lawn outside my house. My baby was walking home from a night club and this animal did it . . . did it to my child on my lawn right under my bedroom window.

Everyone is silent for a moment.

Chalky I don't know what to say.

Paul (*ferociously*) Then shut up, Chalky.

Carl (*up quickly and moving*) More drink. Danny, let's have another drink.

No one moves.

Paul I'll have another drink.

Carl Good. Danny, get more drink.

Paul Thank you.

Danny does as he's told.

Carl It's a disgusting world, Paul.

Paul It's a fucking despicable world, Carl.

Carl How are you sleeping?

Paul I can sleep. I can always sleep.

Danny What did the solicitor say?

Paul I thought they might be able to intervene – you know, get things moving with the police – but they're all just as fucking useless as one another.

Carl There's evidence after something like that. DNA and fibres . . .

Paul I can't wait for that.

Danny arrives back with a bottle of lager, which Paul siezes and takes a swig from.

Carl Understandable. Then there's the question of whether you can trust them. The police, I mean, you know, to get it right.

Paul How do you mean?

Danny (*quiet but urgently*) Leave it.

Paul No, go on.

Carl (*on thin ice here, and he knows it*) I mean, to get all the . . . evidence right, you know, from the lab or whatever. You read about them losing samples and files and . . .

Paul (*shaking his head dismissively*) No, no. Someone will pay. You can't do something like this to a man like me and walk away and have nothing happen to you. It's hanging over them now. If they know me, they know it's hanging over them like a clenched fist.

Chalky What is?

Paul Justice. Like a clenched fist. And if they don't know me, they won't see it coming, but it's still there.

Carl We're all fathers, we all feel the same.

Chalky I'm not, neither's Danny.

Carl (*insistent*) We all feel the same. Lionel?

Lionel I can't say anything. I'm shocked. It's been a day of shocks. First that horse . . .

Paul Horse?

Chalky You weren't there. A horse came through the windscreen of a sports car today.

Paul I missed it.

Lionel You should have seen it. Flesh and blood everywhere. All over the seats –

Carl Alright, Lionel, so the horse is dead – this is something else here. This is a something that's happened to a . . . to a friend of ours.

Paul Thank you, Carl.

Carl Any ideas at all? Any boyfriends or –?

Paul Nothing like that.

Carl No jealous ex-boyfriends?

Paul (*angry*) I've been over it, don't you think I've been all over it?

Carl Of course you have.

Chalky So you put your faith in the police, I suppose.

Paul You fucking joking? (*Beat.*) They're pitiful – worse than that, they're useless.

Carl He's right, of course – you can't necessarily trust the police to get it right.

Paul So let them do what they do and I'll do what I do.

Danny Which is what?

Paul I keep my ear to the ground, Danny, why do you think I'm here? I would of course appreciate it if you did the same.

Carl Course, course we will. Anything to help, Paul. Really.

Paul (*stands up and takes another swig before he pulls his mobile out of his pocket*) Carl, I need to . . .

Carl Use the bedroom. Go in and use the bedroom for privacy.

Paul goes over to the bedroom and steps inside. There is a collective sigh of relief as he disappears and the door closes behind him.

Lionel Bloody hell.

Chalky What do you say? When a man like Paul says that to you, what do you say?

Carl Nothing, you say nothing.

Chalky What's he doing here? You're telling me he's going dog-racing after he's told us all that?

Danny He's not interested in dog-racing. It's not why he's here.

Carl It's exactly why he's here. To take his mind off of it. Life goes on. Paul's that kind of man.

Danny Fucking life goes on? You heard him, he's tranquillising his wife. Doping her up. He belongs at home at a time like this.

Carl It's fine, it's all fine. Just don't say anything without checking it with me first.

Danny What?

Carl It's a sensitive situation. Don't go in with both feet. Check it with me first.

Danny You? You're the one winding him up. You jumped in with both feet on the police-can't-be-trusted line. What was all that about?

Carl I am a host, it's my job to make conversation. Besides, it happens to be true.

Danny And your experience is what? In this particular matter of great miscarriages of justice, your particular experience is what?

Carl I know what I'm talking about. What I read. Look at the Guildford Four. Look at my own divorce.

Danny You and the Guildford Four? Are you even listening to yourself?

Carl (*firmly*) Carole put it one way, and that's the only way the police wanted to hear it. The threat of assault and verbal abuse. That was it in their eyes.

Danny Carl – it's different.

Carl It's evidence, isn't it? There were two versions of a story – they chose to hear hers, not mine. Her evidence, not mine. Mine was equally as valid. I didn't hit her, strike her or whatever. I shouted at her. Well, people shout things they don't mean. Look, my point is, things get clouded – and the police, they can't always see the detail. That's my experience.

Danny Take my advice and keep your experience to yourself. The way he's talking is dangerous. He's a coiled fucking spring –

Carl Exactly, and I think I'm the best judge of how to negotiate this one.

Danny No.

Carl Listen, this should be one of the happiest nights of our life. Chalky? Lionel? We've been waiting for this one to come for months. You know what this dog means to us. It means each of us owning a little piece of something that's been bred to win. To fucking win. And we own it. What do you think of that? (*Pause.*) Lionel?

Lionel (*slowly, with his eyes on the floor*) That's good, that is.

Carl Chalky?

Chalky I just wanted to go dog-racing.

Carl We're going dog-racing. Rick will come up, we'll have a drink all together and then we'll go. Paul knows the significance of tonight, it isn't wasted on him. Just watch what you say, that's all. You heard Danny, he's a coiled spring. (*Beat.*) Follow my lead, I can handle this.

Paul emerges from the bedroom and slips his mobile in his pocket.

Paul She's taken two pills and now she's going to sleep.

Carl Wise, very wise at a time like this. It's a great healer.

Paul What is?

Carl Sleep.

Danny It's time that's a great healer.

Carl Pardon me?

51

Danny That's the expression, 'Time is a great healer.'

Carl Sure, sure, but sleep, I think as the expression goes, is better.

Danny What expression is that, then?

Carl (*annoyed*) Drink, Paul?

Chalky (*quickly*) No. No more drink, for any of us.
I mean, we want to be able to enjoy the race and I think
drink would be bad, getting in the way of enjoying the
race – don't you think, Lionel?

Lionel What is actually in Tia Maria?

Paul I'll have a beer.

Carl Beer and a Tia Maria. Danny?

Danny I'm fine.

Carl Fine, fine.

Lionel (*looks at his watch*) What time do we have to be
there for, then?

Carl I said nine, that's her race time. Rick will be here,
don't panic.

  Pause.

Paul Is he always late?

Danny Who?

Paul Rick.

Danny No.

Paul Just when it matters.

Chalky He's been on holiday, he only got back today.

Paul How is it you know everything?

Chalky I listen. Danny told me. Besides, when I go in the office to order parts I talk to him, and this week he wasn't there. He got a last-minute package deal and he went away, isn't that right, Dan?

Danny He's been away all week.

Chalky (*laughing*) 'When Chalky's dancing, when he's dancing . . .' That's wonderful, that is.

    Small pause.

Lionel He's always going away on holiday, that Rick. And he's always the same when he gets back an' all. A real big-picture man. 'Small world.' 'Makes you think.' I'll give him two weeks before he's playing the lottery and reading his horoscope again along with the rest of us.

    Small pause.

Paul I was supposed to go away again in two weeks. Susan used to be an air hostess before we had the kids, so we get good deals. We'll have to postpone this one.

Carl Of course.

    Pause.

Paul I don't know him.

Lionel Who?

Paul Rick. I don't go in the office. As a matter of fact, I hate the fucking office.

Carl Too true, the phones and the suits and the insurance estimators swanning in and out. I hate it too, Paul. Hate it.

Danny You're in there all the time.

Carl Against my will. I have paperwork to do, you know.

Danny Paperwork?

Lionel They have doughnuts on a Friday.

Carl Who does?

Lionel The office. Rick and Tony and Matt and Tara. They take it in turns to buy each other doughnuts and they have them with their coffee on Fridays.

Carl (*for show*) Now I don't like that.

Danny What exactly don't you like about that?

Carl That's cliquey. That's like them having their own little breakaway group.

Danny It's not like that at all. It's about four people eating doughnuts on a Friday. You could do that. Everybody in their own little section could do that. We could do that in the paintshop, or in the workshop or in the valet bay, but we don't because it takes organisation and lists and 'Whose turn is it?' and 'Sorry, lads, I've forgotten this week.' It would last about five minutes.

    Pause.

Chalky I don't like doughnuts, so it doesn't bother me either way. (*Beat.*) I like the office, it's warm and he sings in there.

Paul Who sings?

Lionel Rick sings. He changes the words in songs.

Chalky (*disappointed*) Does he do that with you as well?

Lionel He does it with everyone. Puts your name in like he's singing it just to you.

Paul (*shaking his head*) I don't like Rick.

Danny (*a knee-jerk reaction*) You just said you don't know him.

Paul I know him.

Danny But you just said you . . . If you knew him, you'd like him. Carl?

Carl Rick, yeah yeah, he's fine. He's fine, Paul. (*Pause.*) Although . . .

Danny Although what?

Carl I don't know him that well myself.

Danny You know him, you speak to him all the time.

Carl That's true, but it's all very surface, all very . . . what's the word – it's polite, it's polite, and that's all with him.

Danny What's wrong with polite?

Carl It's a veneer, Daniel.

Lionel (*to Chalky*) I didn't think I'd have my vocabulary improved going dog-racing.

Chalky Every day is an education, Lionel.

Carl (*feeding this to Danny and Paul*) Politeness is a veneer, a surface. I don't know him because his politeness keeps him at arm's length.

Danny That is bullshit. You knew him perfectly well and liked him until Paul said something different –

Carl (*exposed, he goes further*) Maybe I don't trust him.

Danny What?

Carl There, I've said it. There's something about him.

Danny What?

Carl Danny, I don't want to slag the lad off, he's obviously your friend, but I have to agree with Paul a little bit.

Danny You don't trust him now?

55

Carl Just leave it. It's not a big thing.

Danny No, I won't leave it. Back up what you just said. Come on. (*Beat.*) Come on.

Paul He whispers when he talks to you.

Danny I beg your pardon?

Carl What's that, Paul?

Paul (*turning*) He has a habit of whispering when he talks to you. He stands too close and he whispers what he could just say normally.

Danny What you mean is, he's quietly spoken.

Paul Don't tell me what I mean.

Carl He whispers. I think that's a fair description. Chalky?

Chalky I think he's a great kid. He's just like Gary Lineker is Rick. He's the kind of fella that if you found him in bed with your missus you'd tuck him in and sleep on the couch.

Carl You've obviously never found your wife in bed with another man, Chalky.

Chalky I'm not married. (*He realises.*) Oh, Carl, I'm sorry.

Danny Forget it, Chalky. Carl – leave it alone.

Carl (*twists the knife*) Stood by while she has an affair with a friend, a good friend. A man like you, Chalky, who a person might like to believe is a friend.

Danny Stop it! For crying out loud, you get an opportunity to twist something and you can't help taking it, can you?

Carl He said –

Danny He didn't mean anything by it and you know it.

Chalky I meant that he's a nice kid and all that.

Paul Slimy bastard.

Danny What? Why?

Carl I think what Paul is saying is that it's all the same thing, the whispering, the singing people's names into songs, the hogging doughnuts. It's all a bit under-handed, is that what you mean, Paul?

Paul They don't get their hands dirty in the office. Not a single one of them does.

Carl They don't work with their hands, that's true.

Paul But they don't fix anything – he wouldn't know how.

Danny It's not his job to fix anything.

Paul Gliding about with that fucking ponytail. He ought to fix something, he ought to get his hands dirty once in a while.

Carl Gliding, that's exactly what he does.

Danny It's not his job to do that, he works in the office.

Carl Look, Danny, if he's your friend . . .

Danny He's your friend as well. You asked him to join the syndicate. You asked him to pick up the dog. Why would you do that if he's untrustworthy?

Lionel That's a good point. He's a good arguer. You should have letters after your name, Danny.

Carl (*under pressure*) He lives closest to the kennel, that's why – if you must know. I'm not saying I don't trust him –

Danny You are, that's exactly what you're saying.

Carl Alright, I don't trust him. Alright, there's something about him. I can't put my finger on it. Like when they used to measure people's heads years ago to work out if they were criminals or not –

Danny This just gets better and better.

Carl Like then, you can't put your finger on what it is, there's just something that isn't right.

Paul You should have mentioned this before, Carl.

Carl (*glimpsing what he may have done here*) Well . . . I don't think it's anything to worry about.

Paul I need to know all these little things.

Danny Now wait a second.

Paul How old is he?

Danny He's my age. Let's drop this right now, shall we?

Chalky I like him, you can trust him, can't you?

Paul I can't trust anyone. That's the first thing you realise in a situation like mine.

Chalky Fair enough.

Carl We understand, Paul.

Danny I'm going, this is, this is . . . (*He stands.*) I'm going now.

Paul Sit down.

Danny What?

Carl Danny.

Paul Just a few questions about this friend of yours.

Danny Of ours . . . Carl?

Carl So what is this now, Paul?

Paul Just my ear to the ground and just a few questions.

Danny No way.

Carl (*smoothing things over*) Just a few questions, what does it matter? Danny?

Danny No.

Paul Does he go out in town much? Clubs, does he like clubs?

Danny I like clubs – maybe I did it.

Paul Watch it now, Danny.

Carl Calm down. No one's saying anyone did anything.

Paul Oh, someone did something!

Lionel Answer his questions, Danny, you can argue your way out of it.

Danny Out of what? Out of what?

Carl Quiet.

Paul Clubs? (*Pause.*) Does he like them? (*Pause.*) Carl?

Carl (*appealing to him*) Danny?

Danny From time to time he goes to the club in town and to a few bars.

Paul Fine.

Carl That's fine, you see.

   Pause.

Paul Does he drink at this club and these bars?

   Danny looks to Carl, who gestures that he should answer this.

Danny From time to time.

Paul Much?

Danny (*rolling his eyes*) I don't count his drinks.

Paul Watch it, I said (*Beat.*) Carl?

Carl To eliminate him from Paul's inquiry, Dan, that's all. Look at it that way.

Danny (*he laughs bitterly*) Oh, Paul's inquiry, I see. (*Pause.*) Rick got some decent A-levels, not a GNVQ in sight. He didn't go to university. He worked on his dad's window-cleaning business for eight months while his dad died of cancer and then he got a job at our place. And now he estimates damage on cars that come into the yard after an accident. He lives at home, he drives a Tigra, he goes out at weekends – and yes, he has a drink from time to time. He comes home, he gets up, he goes to work. And that happens over and over again. There is nothing remarkable about him at all.

  Pause.

Carl (*leaning back*) Fine, you see, Dan – that's fine. Thank you.

Danny May I stand down now?

  Pause. Paul looks satisfied. Then he says, almost as an afterthought:

Paul Why did he go on holiday last minute?

Danny What?

Paul Someone said he went on holiday last minute.

Chalky I did.

Paul Why did he do that?

Danny He got a good deal for the week.

Paul (*thinking this through*) There are good deals all the time. There are good deals next week.

Lionel Teletext.

Carl Quite right.

Chalky Giveaway prices. Marbella for two – guess how much?

Carl Shut up, Chalky.

Paul Danny?

Danny What?

Chalky (*whispers to Lionel*) I can't use it – my page-hold button is broken on the remote.

Carl Chalky?

Danny So he went away last minute . . .

Paul Why last week, why not this week?

Danny That's not a question I can answer.

Paul Try.

Danny (*appealing*) Carl?

Carl (*nervous*) Try, Danny.

Danny Why did he go away last week last minute? Let's see – well maybe he was sick and tired of being surrounded by morons at work and he just thought – sod this, I'm off.

Paul (*shaking his head, almost in pity*) He could have chosen any week, but he chose last week. What day did he leave on?

Danny (*nervous*) I'm not saying.

Chalky Saturday.

Danny Shut up, Chalky.

Chalky Sorry, Danny.

Paul Saturday. (*Pause. As if this is conclusive.*) The day after it happened.

Danny That's right, the day after. Just like I drove down the coast the day after and Carl worked on the boat with the kids and Lionel might have had a go at the lawn. Rick went on holiday. None of us knew, Paul, and even if we had . . . (*Pause.*) I'm sorry for what's happened to you and yours, Paul, really I am. But the world doesn't revolve around it . . . (*He realises how bad this sounds, but it's too late.*)

Paul It does, Danny, believe me. The whole fucking lot of it does. Everything round and round brings you back to it. You can't do a thing, there's no, no, not a second of peace or . . . I've got a wife popping pills to sleep. A child who doesn't speak to me, because of what's going on up here – (*Taps his head with his finger.*) God knows what. The whole fucking world is in on it. Don't tell me it doesn't revolve around it, because that's all there is when it's happening to you. (*Pause. He recovers himself a little.*) So I'll ask as many fucking questions as I like if it's all the same to you.

Carl Alright, let's all calm down a bit. Drinks?

Paul Is that alright with you, Dan, or are there any other little pieces of information you're keeping to yourself there?

Danny This is stupid.

Paul This is the very opposite of stupid. This is working it out. Like Carl said, this is eliminating your friend from my inquiries. Am I right, Carl? Carl?

Carl (*nervously*) Right, yes – maybe this is absolutely the way to go.

Paul And I've heard enough to want to hear a little bit more.

The buzzer goes.

Chalky Rick.

Lionel (*standing*) Let's go down.

Paul We're not done up here yet.

Danny This is . . . Look, you work with a person, alongside him, you know him. This wasn't Rick. Come on now? Chalky? Lionel? Brother? Come on now, not Rick, not for a second.

Silence.

Don't let him up, Carl. Don't let him walk into all this.

Paul Sit down. Carl, get the door.

Danny Brother, come on.

Pause.

Carl (*ashamed*) It's alright.

The buzzer goes again. Carl looks between Danny and Paul.

It's eliminating him from Paul's inquiry, Dan, look at it that way. I can handle it, brother.

The buzzer goes once more.

Paul Carl!

Carl walks over to the intercom and presses the button. We hear a voice. Carl overcompensates with a cheery tone, which falls flat.

Carl Hello? Alright, then, come on up then. Has she? Bring her up then. Alright.

He buzzes him in. Carl turns.

(*weakly*) He says the dog's got the jacket on and all that.

Paul steps up into the kitchen and walks straight over to the small table, which he pushes to one side out of the way.

Chalky But what time is it?

Paul There's time. Carl?

Carl There's time, Chalky. Just a few questions, that's all, isn't that all, Paul?

There is a knock at the door. None of the men move. Paul takes a kitchen chair and sets it directly under the naked lightbulb. He looks up.

Paul Ready?

Blackout.

Act Two

*We hear a fist beating on a door. On the third beat the
light from a bedside lamp rises sharply to reveal that we
are in Carl's bedroom.*

*Lionel is half-lounging on the bed, with a piece of
paper in his hand, and the bedside drawer open.*

*Chalky is sitting on the floor at the foot of the bed
inspecting some of Carl's kids' toys strewn about on the
carpet.*

Danny is standing impatiently by the door.

Danny Carl – open the door. Take the chair away and
open the door. Carl! Carl! (*He hammers on the door
again.*)

Lionel (*reading*) 'I wanted to let you know how
delighted I was with the service you recently gave my
Seat Toledo. Phone calls were always polite and helpful
and the repair to my car was excellent. The collection
and delivery were prompt and a clean car was most
acceptable.'

Danny (*pounding on the door again*) Carl! Please, Carl!
(*He bangs again.*) Come on, Carl. Open the door!

Lionel (*still reading*) 'I shall have no hesitation in
recommending you. I am writing to my insurance
company now to tell them of my satisfaction. Sincerely,
Sheila Moore.'

Chalky He looks after those kiddies though, doesn't he?
Look at this lot.

Lionel (*picking through the half-opened drawer*) Isn't it
funny what people keep by their bed? I'm fascinated.

They keep it right here in the closest possible place to where they spend half of their lives and most of the time it's crap. (*He pulls out a woman's scarf.*)

Danny (*hammering on the door again*) Carl – I'll break it down. I swear it. Open the bloody door. Carl! If I keep shouting, the neighbours will call the police. Open the door.

Chalky What are they doing to him?

Danny I can't see. (*Beat. He adds unconvincingly:*) Talking – (*He hammers again.*)

Lionel Then why do they need the door shut, Danny?

Danny Carl's out there, it'll be fine. (*He is out of breath and emotional.*)

Chalky Of course it will. (*Beat.*) Keep knocking, though.

Danny (*pounding on the door*) Carl!

Lionel What time does it start? What race is she in?

Danny That's it, Lionel, keep asking, like a broken fucking record. (*pounding*) Carl!

Chalky We've missed the first two, at least.

Lionel At least. If she's in either of the first two we've had it.

   Danny turns to the other two.

Danny Who's got a phone? Mine's in there. Who's got one? Chalky?

Chalky Who would I call on it?

Danny Lionel? Lionel, get your nose out of my brother's stuff, what's the matter with you?

Lionel (*closing the drawer*) Sorry, Dan, I'm fascinated, that's all.

Danny Take your feet off the bed. Have you got a phone?

Lionel Yeah sure. (*He passes it.*)

Chalky Who are you calling?

Danny (*pauses with his thumb hovering and ready to dial*) I don't know . . .

Chalky Well – what about some back-up?

Danny And who would that be exactly?

Chalky The police – I'd have thought.

Danny And tell them that my own brother is what? Doing what?

Lionel Tell them what's happening.

Danny And call them in on my own brother, and you and all of us?

Chalky Well – we're alright. We haven't witnessed anything.

Danny There's nothing to witness. (*He looks at the phone and then bangs on the door with a flat palm.*) Carl! Please!

Lionel (*shouting from the bed as he folds the letter and replaces it in the drawer*) Come on, Carl, he's worried about Rick. Danny's worried.

> *They stay silent for a second. There is a scratching noise at the door.*

Chalky Listen . . .

Lionel I hear it.

> *Chalky crawls over to the door and scratches back.*

Chalky It's the dog.

Danny It's the fucking dog.

Lionel Like a Rhinestone Cowboy.

Chalky (*scratching back*) Get help, boy.

Danny He's not fucking Lassie. (*Shouts again.*) Carl! Paul!

Chalky You'll scare the dog away.

Danny (*hammering again*) Paul!

   There is silence. Danny sits down on the end of the bed.

Chalky He's good to his kids, isn't he? Look how much all this lot must have cost him.

Danny (*exhausted*) He steals them out of the back of people's cars when he's giving them a wash and a hoover. He cleans them up and he gives them to Caitlin and Steven when they come here at weekends.

Chalky Oh . . . (*He puts down the toy he is holding*) Nice that he thinks of the nippers at work, though.

   Pause.

Lionel Are you late now, Dan?

Danny I'm supposed to be meeting her dad.

Lionel Big step. (*Beat.*) Call her up, if you like.

Danny And what am I supposed to say when she asks where I am?

Lionel (*beat, unsure*) Tell her that you're with your brother.

   A longish pause.
   Danny considers the phone in his hand for a second before tossing it in Lionel's direction.

68

Chalky I'm never sure of your brother, Danny. I never know whether he likes me or not.

Danny (*preoccupied*) He likes you.

Chalky I'm never sure. He gets impatient with me, I think. I don't argue you see. I don't really care about things that he gets so fired up about. I know I should, current affairs and what have you, but I'm just not interested. I should make more of an effort, shouldn't I?

Danny I don't know, Chalky.

Chalky I think so.

Lionel Does your brother smoke in bed? I wondered if I could have a smoke.

Danny Why don't you ask him?

Chalky That's a joke, isn't it?

Danny Yes, Chalky, it is.

Lionel I won't – it's a bit of a slap in the face, smoking in his bed, seeing as he's been such a good host. Well, up until he locked us all in here.

Pause.

How's Bridget, Chalk?

Chalky (*shy*) She's alright. In and out, you know – treats the place like a hotel.

Lionel (*to Danny*) Chalky's got a new lodger called Bridget, who's a divorcee and she's foreign.

Chalky Estonian. Works in an old people's home.

Lionel Chalk's in love, aren't you, Chalk?

Chalky Don't be ridiculous, I'm her landlord.

Lionel Chalk lets her off her rent some weeks.

Chalky Well, she doesn't earn hardly anything.

Lionel Chalky's hoping she might go bowling with him one Friday night if he lets her off the rent for long enough, if you know what I mean?

Chalky Piss off, I do not. Is that what you think?

Lionel Isn't that what you think?

Chalky Danny, that's not in my head at all, honestly. I imagine her as being a stranger in this country and me being a bloody ambassador, if you must know. She's one of the good ones. She works, she's out there earning her keep. She's one of the ones we should be supporting – and that's all I'm doing. Danny?

Danny Chalky, I have no problem with it.

Chalky Thanks, Danny.

Pause.

Danny He can't lock us in a bedroom, he can't do that. I'm his fucking brother. You two are his friends, he has no right. (*He stands and walks toiwarsd the door. Calling through again*) Open the door. (*Beat.*) Unlock the door, open it and let us out. You said two minutes. I am your brother and the door is locked. I'm your fucking brother.

No response. Danny turns and quickly walks over to Lionel. He takes the phone from Lionel's hand and seems to catch his nerve.

Danny (*calls through*) Carl, I've got a phone in here. Carl! I'm saying I might have to call someone. (*Pause.*) It might not take me too long to dial the number, do you understand me? (*Pause.*)

Lionel Go on, son.

Danny is unsure of what to do. He pauses and takes a step back. He looks at the phone but cannot seem to bring himself to dial the number. There is a sound at the door, the men look up. It opens a crack, Carl slips in, closing the door behind him.

Carl (*hushed*) Paul is concerned that all the shouting might panic a neighbour into phoning the police. I told him it's unlikely but that I'd . . . check.

Carl looks at the phone in Danny's hand. All the men's eyes are on it.
Carl quickly takes the phone out of Danny's grasp.

Carl Your phone, Lionel?

Lionel Yeah.

Carl pockets the phone. The men all object noisily. He puts up his hand to silence them.

Danny What are you doing to him?

Carl (*mortified*) Nothing.

Danny Carl!

Carl begins looking for something around the room.

Carl Nothing, honestly – talking. Talking in a civilised way. Going over things. Going over it all.

Danny It?

Carl The crime.

Danny What crime? (*Beat.*) I want to come out there with you.

Carl I know you do – I can hear you and, to be honest, Danny, you're holding things up in there. We can't hear ourselves think.

Chalky He's not hurting him, then?

Carl Look at me. Didn't I say I could handle him – guide him. I'm in control out there.

Lionel Of his temper?

Carl Definitely of his temper, Lionel. Look, let's clear this whole mess up and get on. We've got a dog to race.

Lionel How are we doing for time?

Carl She's not on until nine o'clock, I've said that, Lionel. We're alright for time, we just have to get her settled, see the race marshal, you know, show her off a bit.

Lionel Nine, oh, that's alright – there's time.

Carl Plenty, I'd say – plenty of time.

Chalky Wonderful. How's she doing out there?

Danny watches this conversation in disbelief.

Carl (*smiling*) She's fine. She's trotting around, smelling stuff, you know. Looks good.

Danny How's she doing? Fuck the dog – what has he done to Rick?

Carl Nothing. I've *said* nothing. I'm controlling it, Danny – come on, have a little faith.

Danny In you? You've locked us in your bedroom.

Carl Not locked. I have not locked it. We wedged a chair against the handle, yes, perhaps.

Danny I want to see him.

Carl No.

Danny If I see him, and he's alright – then I'll shut up and I'll let you carry on with your questions.

Carl I can't do that, Dan.

Danny Then how can I believe you when you tell me there's nothing going on out there?

Carl I did suggest you sit with us, but Paul mentioned that it may get in the way of the proceedings.

Danny The proceedings?

Carl And I have to agree with him so far on that. So how about we stop all the distractions, the hammering and shouting? Let's clear this whole mess up, get everything out in the open and get on with tonight . . .

Danny And then what? We'll all go down the track and cheer the dog on?

Lionel Whatever the fucking thing's called.

Carl (*hurt*) Don't say that.

Danny You are threatening a friend of ours.

Carl Of yours.

Danny Of yours, too. Carl, you're behaving like a creature, like a fucking Nazi.

Carl Don't be ridiculous. I'm not a fascist – I'm not political, I'm not even interested in that stuff – I'm just a concerned citizen doing what concerned citizens do – I'm looking after my own. Rick would do the same, to get to the truth – it's the truth we're after.

Danny *This* is what Paul's after.

Carl Not in the grand scheme of things he isn't. Look, it's my night and it's still gonna go fucking well. For me, for Paul, for all of us. He'll want to go to the track, leave it to me. All we want to do is get to the track on time, that is my primary objective here.

Carl takes the scarf from the bedside table.

Danny What's that for?

73

Carl A bandage for him – for Paul. He cut himself, on a cupboard door. (*Pause.*) He punched a cupboard door in the kitchen.

Danny (*standing*) No way – let me out of here!

Carl Danny!

Danny (*shouting*) Open this door now.

Carl For God's sake. It's a bandage for Paul. For Paul.

Danny What's wrong with you!

Carl For Paul, I swear. He got angry and he punched a cupboard door, that's all. And he cut his knuckle and, to tell you the truth, it's going everywhere and that rug is virtually new.

Chalky He cut his own hand, Dan.

Danny Punching a cupboard door. Aren't you listening? Chalky, we're not dealing with a human being here. There's a man out there who broke another man's jaw for taking his parking space.

Carl Dislocated . . .

They all turn to Carl.
Beat.

(*weakly*) He only dislocated it.

Danny (*slow and measured*) This is a big night for you, brother – I know that. You've got us all here – you've got the syndicate's first night and now you're mixing it out there with one of the big boys, helping out Paul – ingratiating yourself –

Carl I don't know what that means.

Danny It means kissing arse, it means trying to mix in higher circles.

Carl And what does it tell you about our chances, if a man like Paul wants in?

Beat.

Danny (*suddenly*) Let Lionel see him.

Carl What?

Danny Take Lionel with you and let him see Rick and then I'll know he's alright.

Carl (*pauses while he thinks about this*) Alright, that'll be alright. Lionel?

Lionel Alright, sure. (*He gets up.*) Alright, Dan?

Danny nods. Carl walks to the door.

Carl Paul, it's me. I'm ready to come out. (*Beat.*) I'm bringing Lionel with me to have a look at Rick, for Dan – to keep him quiet.

Lionel And I need a slash.

Carl And he needs a slash.

The door opens and both Lionel and Carl leave.
Danny takes a step towards it but the door shuts.
Danny and Chalky look at each other.
   Pause.

Chalky I didn't need a slash but now he's mentioned it . . .

   Pause.

Danny (*hesitates*) You want to know the stupid thing? He doesn't even like girls. Rick, I mean –

Chalky Oh, right. (*Beat.*) I didn't know.

   Pause.

I haven't eaten all day on purpose. I had my heart set on a basket meal at the track.

Danny What a fucking mess of a night.

Pause.

Chalky You in love, then?

Danny doesn't look up. After a moment he turns serious.

Danny There's nothing wrong with her, is there?

Chalky Wrong with her, what's wrong with her?

Danny Nothing.

Pause.

Chalky You mean her hips?

Danny What's wrong with her hips?

Chalky Nothing.

Danny Bloody hell.

Pause.
  *The door opens and Lionel comes back in alone.
  The door shuts behind him. Lionel moves silently and
  sits down on the edge of the bed.*
  Pause.

Danny Tell us, then?

Lionel He looks confused, but they haven't touched him.

Danny Is he alright? – I mean is he sat down or . . .
where is he?

Lionel He's in the kitchen. He's sat in the kitchen
and Paul's standing opposite him and they're just talking,
I suppose, although they weren't talking when I walked
through, it was quiet. Paul's hand is bleeding and it's
wrapped in a scarf.

Danny (*to himself*) What have they told him?

Lionel I don't know.

Danny I know, I know – I'm just wondering what they've told him. (*He thinks for a moment.*) What was the expression on Paul's face?

Lionel I don't know – sort of friendly but that could mean anything. (*Pause.*) Your brother seems nervous . . .

Danny shakes his head.

(*troubled*) I'm not sure – I'm not altogether sure he's in charge of the situation, Dan, like maybe he thinks he is.

Dan hangs his head.

Lionel Bathroom's coming on, though. (*He launches himself onto the bed and gets comfortable.*)

Danny paces around before he walks up to the door and knocks on it.

Danny Rick, it's Danny. Paul's got an idea in his head and he's trying to get you to admit to something and it's important that you don't listen to him or admit to anything. Don't listen to Paul. (*Bangs on the door.*) It's Danny. (*Bangs on the door again.*)

Carl bursts in and slams the door behind him.

Carl You are embarrassing me, Daniel.

Danny Step out of the way.

Carl What is the matter with you? You're giving the impression I can't control my own little brother.

Danny You can't, so step out the way.

Carl Listen, listen, are you listening now? That man out there married an air hostess –

Danny How does that matter now, Carl? Start making some sense.

77

Carl Listen to me now, this is everything. (*Up close to Danny and deadly serious.*) He married an air hostess. Paul did. Free air miles – holidays, two, sometimes three times a year. No package deals or bullshit. The fucking works. He's in charge of a workshop of men – couple of clever kids – normal kids. A games room extension which he built, and now a stake in a greyhound. Well, if someone came along to take that away from you – you'd put up a fight.

Danny Carl listen to me. You are not in control of this any more, this is out of hand now.

Carl You're wrong, Dan, you haven't seen me out there. He's listening to me.

Paul walks in quickly and quietly and shuts the door behind him. He stands squarely in front of it so no one can think of leaving.

Danny (*stepping forward*) I want to speak to Rick.

Paul You can't.

Danny Why?

Paul You just can't. You'll fuck up the sensitive balance.

Lionel What does that mean?

Paul It means I think he's close to saying something.

Danny What's he gonna say –?

Paul He'll tell me something.

Danny And what will that be worth if you've beaten it out of him?

Paul Carl!

Carl Now, now. We haven't touched him – we haven't! Paul hasn't laid a finger on him, in fairness – and under very difficult circumstances.

78

Danny Where's the scarf? You had a scarf wrapped around your –

Paul shrugs. Danny waits a moment before taking a step towards the door. Paul sidesteps to block him.

Paul We're all in here, Danny. He'd have run out otherwise –

Carl What have you done then, Paul?

Paul Tied his hands.

Mutters of disagreement.

Chalky (*standing up*) No, now come on. Fair's fair.

Lionel Tied his hands? You said just talking!

Carl (*desperate, feeling the room turning*) Well, I suppose . . . in hindsight it's no more than a prank someone might pull on a stag night, you know, as a joke.

Danny Jesus, Carl.

Danny looks at Carl. Carl drops his eyes.
  Pause.
  After a moment or two Danny turns and faces Lionel, realising his position and quiet seniority in the room.

Lionel –

Danny walks over to where Lionel is sitting and kneels respectfully next to him.

(*in hushed tones*) That is Rick out there and his hands are tied up to stop him from getting away. Lionel? Haven't we seen enough blood for one day? Lionel, with the horse and . . .?

Danny Look at me, Lionel.

Lionel (*beat*) Nobody knows who their neighbours are any more.

Danny (*angry at not getting his support*) What does that matter, Lionel, really?

Lionel It's a good thing to know. You should know. Look at this wall here. (*to Carl*) You sleep a foot away from yours and I bet you don't know their first names even. It's where it starts. You don't say hello to your neighbours and the next step is not giving a shit about your neighbours –

Danny And then tying them up with a scarf.

Lionel I don't know anything about that.

Danny Listen, Paul. I don't know what to say, only that I'm sorry for what's happened to you and yours.

Paul You've said that once already – that doesn't sound so sincere, Dan.

Danny Well, I mean it. But he is a friend, if not of yours then of mine, and I am asking you for a favour. As a man that my brother respects.

Paul Not you, Dan? No respect from you?

Danny (*faltering*) I'm asking that we go and untie Rick and come back to all this on another day when we've all just had a breather.

Paul (*slowly shaking his head*) My child –

Danny I know, but it doesn't give you licence to do this to another person, who is your friend, who you work with. Has he got the first idea why he's tied to a fucking kitchen chair? Paul, really, has he?

Paul (*closing in on Danny*) My baby.

Carl (*coming between them*) He understands we're fathers here too, Paul, if anyone touched my little girl, did anything like that to her, I don't know what I'd do.

Danny But not this, Carl, you wouldn't do this.

Everybody stares at Carl, including Paul. He realises this is a crux moment. Carl looks around and picks his words carefully.

Carl If someone touched . . . my little girl . . .

Chalky Rick wouldn't be interested in that.

Beat.

Paul What?

Carl What's that, Chalky?

Chalky (*beat*) Dan?

Paul You're always talking, aren't you? Say that again!

Chalky, who is sitting in a heap on the floor, looks at Danny. Danny shakes his head. Chalky looks back to Paul, and hesitantly shakes his.
   Paul stands and takes a few steps towards Chalky.

Paul I need to know everything. (*Beat.*) Now say that again. (*He steps closer to Chalky.*) Go on, say it again.

Danny Leave him.

Paul Don't do that – don't hold out on me. Say it again!

Carl (*beat*) He's an idiot, Paul, don't listen to a word.

Paul is standing right over Chalky now. Chalky draws his feet and hands into his body and is now in a tight ball on the floor.

Paul Tell me what you said. I need to know it all. (*Beat.*) Say it again! (*shouting*) Chalky, say it again!

Paul is towering over him now. Chalky covers his face. Paul draws back his foot.

Danny (*can't take it any more*) Rick doesn't like girls is what he said.

Lionel Fucking hell.

Paul Is that right, Chalky?

Chalky is shaking on the floor.

Danny It's alright, Chalk. (*Beat.*) Paul, he didn't do this, Rick doesn't like girls. He shouldn't be tied up out there. He doesn't even like girls!

Beat.

Paul It wasn't the girl. (*Beat.*) It was my boy David.

There is a long pause while they all take this in.

Do you know what they do? What they get up to these queers? They stick fucking fingers and thumbs up each others arses, in toilets. In our public toilets. Fingers up arses. (*Beat. He is suddenly conscious of himself.*) I've got to get on.

Paul walks out slamming the door.
  Pause.

Carl Didn't I say? You don't say anything without checking it with me first? Danny, you heard me say that.

Danny steps over to Chalky, who has his hands over his eyes and is shaking a little, not realising he is out of danger. Danny steps over to him and puts his hand on his shoulder. Chalky flinches and uncovers his face to see Danny standing where Paul was. Chalky is breathing heavily.

Danny Alright?

Chalky I'm not ashamed to admit I was scared. I'm not bothered, I'm just saying. (*He looks at Danny.*) Thank you.

Carl (*sarcastically*) Think nothing of it, Chalk.

Chalky Oh, and thank you, Carl. I heard you talking at one point. I didn't hear what you said though, but thank you.

Lionel What a day. What happened to the way today was supposed to work out?

Danny (*to Carl*) You have to get out there.

Carl Right, now I've got to think.

Danny Son? Daughter? What does this change? Nothing.

Carl (*looking at his watch*) Okay – I suggest –

Danny No. No more suggestions.

Carl Danny, you'll be grateful I'm working out the angles on this one – don't you want to get out of here?

Danny Rick is tied to a chair. Go and untie him and let him go.

Chalky (*whispering*) The son was raped, how does that happen? It's not possible, surely.

Lionel Do you think it could be the boy who's at hairdressing college? I mean, do you think the boy could be queer?

Carl Right, you see – that sort of comment simply won't do, Lionel. (*pointing at the door*) The man's blood is up. Don't go saying things like that.

Danny You started this. You let him think Rick couldn't be trusted.

Carl Oh, Danny, will you give it a rest? We've moved beyond that now and I'm doing my best to keep everyone up to speed because to tell you the truth this situation is turning into something of a minefield.

Chalky (*earnestly*) What do you suggest, Carl?

Carl Well, for starters, let's not mention that Paul's boy might be, you know . . .

Lionel (*whispers*) What? A shirt-lifter?

Lionel, Chalky and Carl titter a little.

Carl (*laughing*) Ssh, stop it now.

Lionel A Marmite-miner. An uphill gardener.

Carl A pillow-biter.

Chalky A chutney-ferret.

Carl (*still laughing*) Ssh, serious now, he'll fucking go for you.

Lionel Be funny, though, wouldn't it? For big old Paul, old Punchy Paul, to have a queer son. Wouldn't that be funny?

Danny I'm sure it's fucking hilarious for the queer son.

Carl (*serious*) So look, that's enough of that, I think. For safety sake.

Chalky Don't worry – not another word out of me.

Carl Lionel?

Lionel (*beat*) I was just trying to think of some more.

Carl (*happy*) Was I or was I not right in saying that he has always been a peculiar fella. Fucking unbelievable. Well, this changes things . . .

Danny How?

Carl Oh, very much so, yes indeed.

Danny How?

Carl Well, you tell me, Dan – but isn't it just a bit too much of a coincidence that the guy we've suspected all along suddenly became prime suspect?

Danny (*annoyed by his logic*) I'm sorry, I don't really follow. Rick is a prime suspect now?

Carl Now he is, yes, of course.

Lionel A sexual deviant.

Danny Deviant?

Carl (*smugly*) He's deviated from the normal sexual path, by going with fellas – therefore, yes, I think it is fair to say that he is a sexual deviant and we all know what they are capable of. (*Pause.*) Read the papers, switch on the news.

Danny Okay, listen. You like women, but you would never attack one, or hurt one, take advantage of one. But you like women.

Carl (*weary*) I see where this is going.

Chalky This is a good point. Go on, Danny.

Danny It doesn't make Rick a person who would attack another person.

Carl And the dates, the last-minute holiday?

Danny That doesn't mean a thing. It's important that we realise that who he is or what he likes doesn't make him a sexual deviant.

Lionel I thought we'd established that he was a sexual deviant.

Danny He's half the fucking size of Paul's boy.

Lionel That's true.

Danny He couldn't attack him, not at half the size.

Chalky That's true, Carl.

Danny Carl, promise me. Promise me you won't go out there and say something that could wind up with someone innocent getting seriously hurt. Someone who's tied to a chair and can't defend himself. In your home. On your rug.

Carl Danny, please, I'm trying to think.

Danny (*a last-ditch effort*) They won't let the kids come and visit, you know. The police won't. Not in a house where there's been violence. A disturbance of the peace.

Carl stares at him. He is silent and worried.

Danny The eyes of the law wouldn't see you as a fit father if you were an accessory to anything like that. Brother, it's true. If they found out –

Carl Well, they wouldn't.

Danny If anything happened here tonight and they found out . . . there's a chance they'd keep the kids from you. There's a chance, Carl. That means you're gonna have to do something about this.

Paul enters again quietly while the gravity of this sinks in for Carl.

Paul What are you doing? I need you out here, Carl, he's calmer with you around.

Carl (*turns*) Yeah, sure. I was just . . .

Paul turns to leave.

. . . discussing.

Paul What?

Carl faces Paul.

Carl Homosexuality. (*Beat.*) Stuff to do with gays.

Paul (*pause*) What stuff?

Carl Whether what they get up to is . . . could be classed as deviant.

Paul As what?

Carl Deviant, different, wrong or something.

Paul stares at Carl suspiciously for the first time.

Paul You've just answered your own question.

Paul goes to walk out. Carl steps over to the door and blocks him.

Carl I'm just thinking that maybe we don't know what we're dealing with now, do we? It isn't so straightforward now. I mean Rick is . . . (*turning to Danny*) Well, he's not a very big lad, is he?

Paul I haven't got time for this.

Carl Only, when I thought it was your daughter that got, you know . . . then I thought maybe, with the holiday and the dates and . . . but now it's the son, and not the daughter, and what with Rick not being very big . . . it's just that your David is a big lad, he could see Rick off . . . if he really wanted to.

Paul If?

Carl Well . . .

Paul (*pause*) I looked out my bedroom window and saw it all. Can you fucking imagine that? Looking down at your front lawn and seeing an animal doing that to your own son.

Danny (*softly*) It wasn't Rick.

Paul I opened the front door and he ran – got up off my front lawn and disappeared. Left my boy just sitting there in the wet grass. I must have seen a face – why can't I remember a fucking face?

Danny You know it wasn't him.

Paul (*pure hatred*) He's one of them, isn't he?

Danny And that's enough, is it?

Paul It's enough for starters.

Danny What are you going to do?

Pause. Silence.

Carl (*brave face*) Talk, talk it out. Talk it out in the open, get it all ironed out – right, Paul?

Pause. Paul refocuses on Carl.

Paul I'm disappointed in you, Carl. I had you down for more than just a talker.

Paul looks Carl straight in the eye, his blood is boiling now. Carl is blocking his way. For a moment neither man moves. Paul's stare becomes more intense and Carl begins to waver.

You're either out there with me or you're standing in my way.

Carl holds it for as long as he can but it is too much for him. He breaks the stare and stands to one side.

Carl Make it quick, we've got a dog to race.

Paul exits as Danny rises to follow. The door shuts before Danny can get to it.

(*mortified*) Disappointed, he said.

Danny (*astonished*) You choose the fucking dog?

Carl Did you see the way he looked at me? Disappointed, he says.

Danny I can't believe you choose the fucking dog over somebody tied to a chair.

Carl I've been a friend to Paul. Made him a part of this syndicate. I mean . . . I'm the voice of reason out there.

A stifled scream comes from the other side of the door. Everybody looks up. No one moves or speaks for a few moments.

Suddenly Danny jumps up and runs over to the door. He tries the handle but it won't open. He turns nervously to the other three, who stare back, dumbstruck. Lionel jumps up and runs to the door and begins pulling on the handle. Chalky quickly steps over, so now all three are trying with all their might to get the door open, while Carl sits crumpled on the bed.

After trying for some moments, Lionel and Chalky stop. Danny tries fruitlessly on his own, before giving up and eventually leaning against the door. Silence.

Carl (*oblivious*) I didn't fight for custody of my two. It wouldn't have been a fight, would it? And still I think I should have –

Danny Carl? (*softly*) Carl! There's a telephone in your pocket.

Carl – made a stand or something. Showed their mother and everyone else that they were my blood and that meant something, even though everyone said it would be better off for them to be with her. Though it is, I'm sure it is.

Danny Carl? We've got to call somebody now.

Carl And then there's Paul, out there fighting for his family.

Danny No.

Carl Yes. Fighting for them as we speak. Not talking about it, fighting. And I think that – I just think that if everyone felt that way . . . cared as much as that . . . and would never let anything happen to one of their loved ones because if it did there is no limit to what they'd do . . . If we all felt that way, well then, I wonder if we'd be in the shit we're in now.

Danny This isn't about that, Carl.

Carl Isn't it?

Danny This is about a man who caught his own son in the middle of the night fucking another man on his front lawn and he can't bear to think about what that means. What that might make his own son. (*Pause.*) Use the phone, Carl. He could be doing anything out there and you can stop it. You have to.

Carl (*distant*) I was imagining hearing the dog's name over the tannoy. Watching people's reactions. Maybe telling a few people: 'She's ours.' 'Quick dog,' somebody would say. 'Thank you very much, feel free to have a flutter. I think she's got a chance in this one.'

Danny Brother, please!

Carl And they'd take it all in, give me a wink and walk over to the Tote and put a fiver on Sharkey's Necklace to win. So now that fella's cheering her on as well. Not just us, it's him now and maybe someone else and then another and so the circle grows.

Danny (*shouting*) Carl!

Carl (*turning bitter*) You don't even recognise the name, do you?

Danny What?

Carl The name! The reason why it's significant?

Danny Give me the phone.

Chalky What does the name mean, Carl?

Carl It means something significant. Danny, why don't you tell them?

Danny Not this again, Carl, not now. Please give me the phone?

Carl It was our father's nickname.

Danny Fine, it was his nickname. The phone!

Carl Don't patronise, me you little shit. They'd stopped calling him that by the time you were born. Sharkey, they used to call our dad Sharkey.

Lionel Who did?

Carl Who did, Danny?

Danny Everyone did, Carl, is that what you want me to say?

Carl He wore a necklace of shark's teeth. One of the only ones I'd ever seen. Wore it for years. Married my mum in it. His dad brought it back from the Seychelles. There were stories that went with it. One time the string broke and these bloody teeth went everywhere – scattered all over the kitchen floor. I was still finding them months later. So he didn't have a necklace any more and he didn't have a nickname or any stories.

Chalky Why?

Carl Because he didn't have a necklace any more.

Chalky What did people call him?

Carl I don't know, his name – if they knew his name. He wasn't a remarkable man at all. He was very easy to pass over, except in that necklace and then all of a sudden he didn't have it. We don't talk about him, do we, Dan?

Danny Carl, please!

Carl And I think that's terrible. I mean, he's our father after all. He wasn't a bad man, he was just a dull man who died one day.

Lionel So the dog is a, sort of a –

Chalky Tribute.

Carl No, a reminder. I am not my father's son. (*Pause.*) You don't pass me over. I'm more than just talk, I am, much more. Look at all this, a dog, a syndicate. That's not talk – that's happening before our very eyes. That's not nothing, you know.

Danny Have you finished telling stories? Can I have the phone now?

Carl He was your father too, Danny.

Danny No one called him Sharkey, you made it up when we were kids, brother. He was a dull man who had a necklace that may or may not have been made of shark's teeth, I don't know, but the rest is bullshit and you know it.

Carl It is not bullshit.

Danny There is not an ounce of truth to that story. I'm sorry, but there isn't.

Carl (*desperate*) There is, an ounce. The name is significant, it has to be.

Danny The name is nothing. It means nothing. Now we need to use the phone and put this right.

Carl Danny!

Danny (*shouting*) You don't explain away that huge fucking chip on your shoulder by making up stories. It's pathetic. We're dull and that's that.

Carl sits impassively looking back at Danny.
  Pause.

Chalky (*nervously*) Well, I think that's really nice, Carl.
A lovely story . . . the name . . . and it being your dad's
name and . . . and well, maybe you should give Danny
the phone now.

Carl Lionel? What do you think of the name now?

Lionel I think you should do something. I think he could
be doing anything to that boy. It's clear he isn't listening
to you any more.

Carl (*stands*) That's clear, is it, Lionel?

Lionel You're locked in the bedroom with us now.

Carl I'm not locked, there is no lock.

Lionel Well, we can't get out and you're in here with us.
You're supposed to be the voice of reason and you're in
here with us. Besides, it's my phone.

Carl (*taking the phone from his pocket*) You'd ring the
police on this? Call them in on a friend?

Lionel He's no friend of mine.

Danny He's no friend of yours either, Carl, come on now.

Carl Sod the lot of you – I like the man. (*angry*) He gets
things done. You lot, you're not fit to judge a man like
him. All of you are leant on, compromised. (*to Chalky*)
Do you really think that foreign bit in your spare room
is the slightest bit interested in you? She's using you, for
Christ's sake. You're a soft touch – wake up, take a look
at yourself. Look at Lionel, another fucking doormat,
I mean, for crying out loud, stop having babies, is that
too easy for you? Danny's going the exact same way
marrying a cripple. And out there we've got someone

93

who nobody walks over and you say *he's* the one in the wrong. We're the wrong ones.

Danny She is not a cripple. (*deeply angered*) Give me the phone.

Carl Oh, take the fucking phone.

> *He holds it out. Danny snatches it and looks at the other two.*
> *A beat later Danny is ready to use it and Carl is suddenly frightened.*

Dan don't! Don't be a child, Dan. Do you want to be unpopular, Danny, seriously unpopular? Danny? Daniel? I'm your brother, please. He's disappointed enough.

> *Lionel steps forward and stops Carl moving towards Danny.*

Lionel Don't, Dan. (*Pause.*) I'll call them.

Carl What?

Lionel (*taking the phone*) I'll do it.

Carl (*trying to bluff Lionel out of it*) Come on now. You know the man, you work with Paul.

Lionel (*defiant*) What's he gonna do to me?

Carl All sorts, maybe all sorts.

> *Lionel fingers the phone for a moment. He looks down.*

Lionel I'd like to have been a bit more like you, Danny, growing up.

Carl (*exasperated*) Lionel! . . . this isn't appropriate now.

Lionel You wanna listen to this one, Carl. (*Points at Danny.*) He's got more sense than the rest of us put together. (*He fingers the phone again shyly.*) He's smart.

He cares, like a person ought to. (*Beat.*) What's the number?

Chalky It's the same it's always been.

Lionel I thought they had a different number now.

Chalky It's the same. (*Beat.*) They have a non-serious crime number, if it's, you know, non-serious.

Lionel What sort of serious is this, then?

Danny *Serious*, Lionel.

Lionel Course it is. (*Lionel hesitates. He smiles nervously.*) I've never called the police before . . .

Pause. Lionel is genuinely afraid of stepping over the line.

Danny (*sympathetically*) It's okay. If you want me to . . . (*Beat.*) It's fine . . . Lionel.

Lionel looks at him with real affection and smiles.

Lionel Sorry, Dan. I want to do it, but there's a line in the sand, you know, and I've never . . .

Danny Sure.

Lionel hands him the phone and takes a step back. Danny dials 999 slowly and we hear each beep. He lifts the phone to his ear. He waits and then he looks at the phone before putting it back to his ear.

No signal, no fucking signal. Lionel. What is this, Lionel?

Lionel Give it here . . .

Lionel takes the phone and waves it around.

No signal.

Chalky This is why I don't bother with them, for exactly this reason. No signal, why? Why on earth?

Danny Shut up, Chalky.

Chalky I thought computers were supposed to assist you?

Lionel gets up on the bed and holds the phone above his head.

Lionel It's not a computer, it's a mobile phone.

Chalky Well, it's got a computer in it, hasn't it?

Carl Off the bed, off the bed!

Danny Any luck? Lionel?

Lionel jumps down and looks at Danny.

Lionel Sorry, Dan.

Danny runs up to the door, and kicks and hammers on it in a frenzy. The other men look at him, not knowing what to do as he works himself into an almost hysterical state. Finally he slides down the door and hammers on the floor in sheer frustration. Carl walks up to him and touches him on the shoulder. Both men are emotional.

Carl (*whispering*) We've still got the dog.

Danny Don't – don't you dare.

Carl I had a home. I had fucking possessions that matched once. I've been abandoned here, not her, me. And she broke the rules, not me.

Danny This dog, this fucking dog is about winning it all back, everything you seem to think has been taken away from you. She crosses the line first and then what?

Pause.

Chalky (*slowly*) I'm not sure I'm in the mood for racing tonight, Carl, I'm sorry about that.

The men are all silent for a second before they hear a scratching sound at the door. The door suddenly opens and Paul walks in with a beautiful greyhound on a lead. The dog has a jacket on with 'Sharkey's Necklace' embroiderd on the side. Danny races out of the open door. Paul doesn't make an effort to stop him.

Paul He's gone, before you ask. I let him go.

Pause.
Danny walks back in, holding the scarf in his hand.

Lionel We heard him.

Paul What did you hear?

Danny Him, screaming.

Chalky You didn't do anything, did you?

Paul I didn't say that. I said I let him go. I did plenty.

Danny What?

Paul doesn't respond.

I said . . . What did you do?

Paul It occurred to me that he ran away like a hare on a rail, didn't he, girl? (*Pets the dog.*) Anyway, it appears he doesn't want to be a part of our syndicate any more. Which leaves an opening . . . (*Paul looks at Danny.*)

Chalky What did you say?

Paul (*with real venom whilst still petting the dog*) I told him that he should crawl back to his little gay posse and enjoy one last night of being able to sing all his fucking queer little songs because come tomorrow morning nobody's gonna want to hear them any more. I told him it would be advisable to look over his shoulder for as long as he worked with normal working men who didn't

97

go around behaving like greasy little queers. I told him that come tomorrow morning the world is going to seem like a very lonely place. (*to Chalky*) Is that all right, Chalky? Would you like to have added anything to that?

Chalky No.

Paul Good. (*Pause.*) She's been very well behaved, haven't you, darling? (*He kneels down and strokes the dog.*) There was an accident with the rug but –

Carl Sure, never mind.

Paul I've got to say, this name . . .

Carl (*defeated*) Yeah?

Paul (*laughing lightly*) This fucking name! It's got to go, Carl. I'm impressed with the jacket and all that. If it could be unpicked – the lettering, then we could still use the jacket, but the name? It's wrong. Has to be something that says speed.

Lionel Rhinestone Cowboy.

Paul Not right, but more like it. I'll have a think.

Carl What's she chewing?

Paul stands.

She shouldn't eat before a race.

Chalky moves over to the dog and opens her mouth. Something falls on the carpet. Chalky picks it up and looks at it before panicking and throwing it across the room.

Chalky It's a fucking finger.

All the men look at Paul and he stares back.

Paul You didn't ought to let her chew that, Carl. You don't know where it's been.

Pause.

Cheer up, fellas. If you're gonna be like this every fucking Thursday, I think I'd rather go on my own.

Paul exits with the dog trotting behind him. All the men look at the finger on the other side of the room.

Chalky Carl? Are you alright, Carl?

Carl (*haltingly and with a crack in his voice*) I'm very excited, Chalky, very excited. I've been looking forward to this night for months. We're alright, we're on time. I didn't have an itinerary but if I did, we'd be alright – we'd be running to schedule. We'll get to the track, have a look around, meet the race marshal, have a basket meal, just relax . . . drink it in. You see, they don't know what's coming yet, not yet they don't. This dog, our girl, they're not expecting her to win. We'll never have that secret weapon again, so just enjoy it. The minute she crosses that line first, it'll be like the whole world has changed for us . . . you might want to think about that a little bit before it happens.

Danny steps over to the corner of the room, kneels and picks up Rick's finger, which he puts gently in his coat pocket.
He stands with his head down and without looking at the other men.
Pause.

Lionel (*looking at Danny*) I'll see you, Danny. (*Beat.*) Sorry.

Chalky (*to Carl*) We'll leave it for this week then, shall we, Carl? The dogs . . . all things considered?

Beat.

Lionel I'll see you tomorrow, Carl.

Lionel nods and leaves.

Chalky (*to Danny, pointing at his pocket*) You ought to pop that in the freezer – stop it from going bad.

> *Chalky leaves the room slowly.*
> *Carl and Danny both have their eyes set on the floor. Danny has his hands in his pockets while Carl is slightly hunched.*

Carl (*without looking up*) You ought to give that girl of yours a ring.

Danny I will.

Carl You'll have to bring her over one Thursday night. I'll cook. Something half-decent, though.

Danny (*shaking himself out of it*) Look – I can't do this now. I've got to . . .

Carl I'm no good. I know that, Dan, I'm aware of it. We used to set each other straight, you and I. Set me straight, brother. Help me out. Come on now, I'm asking.

Danny Okay. (*Beat.*) You are a coward, brother. You ought to know that. That ought to be what you take away with you after tonight is long gone. You could have stopped this.

Carl You don't stop a man like Punchy Paul, you stand to one side.

Danny There was a moment when you could have. You, you could have.

Carl No, Danny, there wasn't.

Danny You know something? You're just like Dad. You're Sharkey's boy, after all.

Carl And what are you? Marrying a girl from a corner shop, spray-painting cars, with your brains, your natural talent.

Danny I'm just like him too, brother . . . I am.

Danny leaves quietly.

Carl Don't say that, Dan, not these things, not to yourself and not to me. It's the dog, it's all wrapped up in the dog. Something new, a chance to be different, to have something pure and fast.

Carl doesn't turn around – he knows Danny is gone. The lights fade.